Return by Water

surf stories and adventures

Kimball Taylor

Dimdim Publishing
San Diego, California

For information, please contact Dimdim Publishing,
P.O. Box 7362, San Diego, Ca. 92167.
www.dimdimpublishing.com

Although the author and publisher have made every effort to ensure the accuracy and
completeness of information contained in this book, we assume no responsibility for errors,
inaccuracies, omissions, or any inconsistency herein. Any slights of people, places, or
organizations are unintentional.

First printing 2005

Printed in Canada

ISBN 0-9765381-0-5

Library of Congress Control Number: 2005900406

ATTENTION CORPORATIONS, UNIVERSITIES, COLLEGES, AND PROFESSIONAL ORGANIZATIONS:
Quantity discounts are available on bulk purchases of this book for educational, gift purposes,
or as premiums for increasing magazine subscriptions or renewals.

Special books or book excerpts can also be created to fit specific needs. For information,
contact Dimdim Publishing, P.O. Box 7362, San Diego, Ca. 92167; ph 619-223-5891.

Return by Water is dedicated to my family: Brad, Colette, Ian, Cameron, Emily and Lisa.

Special thanks to Eric Blehm, Steve Hawk and Evan Slater, who all had a hand in putting me on this road. I'd also like to thank *Return by Water*'s designer, Shawn Bathe; editor, Rebecca Nordquist and world-famous photographer Grant Ellis, whose image of Dungeons in South Africa graces the cover.

Return by Water

Contents

Author's Note

MOST SURF TRIPS won't readily offer up stories. You travel, score good waves or not, and return home—either happy just for the salt in your hair, or miserably bent over the toilet with a foreign parasite turning your guts inside out. However the trip comes off, when your friends ask you how the trip was, you'll always say it was good, great even.

You won't find that kind of surf trip in this book. Of my easiest surf trips, I remember the flying fish, the odd sea cow, the atmosphere and the waves. I don't write about them. Only trouble makes for good stories, and every story in this book contains something of that crucial storytelling element. Somehow, I've found plenty of trouble on the road, usually the kind my sheer ignorance has created.

Return by Water traces my path from surfer to writer to traveler and, finally, traveling surf journalist. Several of the stories are the result of surf magazine assignments. The title story of this collection is based on a string of factual events, but it remains a work of fiction. For me, it symbolizes the kind of event that takes place at home, yet subconsciously pushes a surfer out into the world, and onto that well-documented pilgrimage. The following stories are the chronicle of such a pilgrimage. —Kimball Taylor

Return by Water

THE NEWSPAPER MENTIONED that she'd been dead 18 hours, the art store girl. So that's a night, a drizzling morning and into the first of a clear afternoon that she'd been missing. Onshore winds eased off briskly approaching dusk that day, and before the sun hinted it might sink down, several big clouds came out of the north and sat on the horizon. The kelp bed began about two miles out and stretched along the coastline like a wide, green oil slick. It was on the inside edge of the kelp bed, the lobster fisherman said, that he noticed the strangest thing he'd ever seen a group of birds do. Ten or 11 seagulls floated around a disembarked patch of kelp and sea grass. With a dying wind, a settling ocean chop and those big clouds waiting out there on the horizon, it looked to the fisherman as if the gulls had sat down to watch the sunset. In hindsight, the fisherman said, the gulls were probably just tending the woman's body, which floated intertwined in kelp leaves and sea grass just beneath the surface. After raising his lobster traps, the fisherman's curiosity pressed him to probe the mass of flotsam with a gaff. The gulls backpedaled from the lunging hook. The large clouds at the horizon shifted in urgent hues of red. By 6:14 p.m., the sun had vanished, reds and oranges chasing after it, and at 6:17, the lobster fisherman discovered the art store girl's nude, mutilated body.

"Red skies at night, you know how they say, sailor's delight. And that's how I was feelin'," the fisherman was quoted in the paper. "Then I found the girl. Sad thing, really."

When the story broke in our local newspaper, her body had gone unidentified for 48 hours. An autopsy was performed, the paper said, and the county medical examiner noted that something had severed her left leg above the knee. Various other tears spotted her flesh. The examiner called them "unusual." With the exception of two rings, a bracelet, a flower tattoo and a mole-removal scar, the body was naked. The examiner also described a fracture in her neck similar to injuries caused by car wrecks. "She is a daughter to somebody," he was quoted in closing. "We hope she is identified soon." That morning, hikers found a small black purse at the base of the cliffs just above the tide pools. Identification inside the purse belonged to 5-foot-7-inch Samantha Rae of St. George, Utah.

"THE WATER'S CHILLY," I said. "A 59-degree skinny dip?"

"She was chummed," Miles said. "Chummed for sure. That's how the mob does it. First they kill you, shoot, strangle, stab. Then they drag your body behind a boat just like trolling for yellowtail. When something attacks, if it's sharks, they slow the boat down so your body gets chewed real good, and then they release." Miles and I leaned against my mustard-colored truck parked at a lookout above the cliffs. Hard white sunlight refracted from the ocean's surface. The ocean's glare forced me to squint while waiting for another set. We watched five waves file in at the horizon, bulging up just inside the kelp bed and warming to a pale blue before folding into foam. Miles shaded his face with a newspaper he'd bought for the tide charts—the paper that reported, incidentally, the identification of Samantha Rae's body.

"There's no sharks out there. The last shark attack happened in 1942," I said repeating something I heard in town.

Below the parking lot, a chest-high field of dandelion rose and fell, carpeting the cliff's furrowed edge. This is the most beautiful time here, spring. Half winter days, half summer. What are normally weeds in chalky tan soil become a thousand eyes of yellow and white. I could smell the pollen and coitus, and the chalky dirt, too, familiar and bittersweet.

"Remember the tiger shark out at In-Betweens? It jumped 2 feet out of the water," Miles said, the skin under his eyes taut over his cheek bones and spotted with sun marks.

"I didn't see it."

"What else would chew your leg off to the knee?" he grinned. "Unless, it was hacked off."

"By boat, the harbor is 45 minutes away. You're saying the Mafia kills an art store clerk, loads her body into a boat, drags it through the channel and dumps it out here?" I asked. "What about the purse?"

Miles winced. "Planted," he said.

Miles had bought brushes from Samantha at least once,

Yasutomo watercolor brushes. I'd gone with him. Now he said he couldn't remember Samantha, but he'd talked about her the same way he talked of other women. "Have you seen the redheaded art store girl?" he once asked. "With the slightly gapped teeth and sleepy eyes. Oh, I love her." He loved all the young girls in town. "I die every time I see one," Miles would say. He often talked of painting women he met or had seen on the street. Of all the sirens who caused Miles these small deaths, though, he painted only the ocean and these cliffs: earthen, brown, horizontally streaked and golden, like sun-kissed hair.

"I'm going home until the tide drops," he said.

I changed into my wetsuit next to my little truck. Sunshine warmed the black neoprene on my back, and I thought about how, as soon as I paddled out, the suit would fill up like a cold water bottle. Down the trail, I walked through shoulder-high flower stalks, the chalky dirt sliding up between my toes. A footpath is worn into the sandstone cliffs making steps that feet fit into perfectly. At the bottom, a small beach ran between the base of the cliff and the intertidal zone, a smooth, blond ribbon. The tide covers and exposes this beach twice a day. When the tide slips out faster than usual, it leaves creatures and sea trinkets shelved on the beach. At times there is a yard sale of crab shells, smashed lobster traps, fish heads, skeletons, sea cucumbers, sand dollars and sea glass. Fiberglass slabs from smashed boat hulls wash in now and again, hanging around for a few days until somebody hauls it up

the cliff. Once, what looked like an entire bamboo forest washed
up in the night and covered the beach. Bamboo will blow out of
river estuaries when flash floods run their course to the ocean.
One morning after a recent storm, I stopped to look over the
bamboo thicket from the top of the trail. A jogger lady ran up
behind me, stopped and asked where it all had come from.
"Washed in from Japan...on the Humboldt current," I said,
looking over my shoulder.

"That's amazing," she said. "There's so much of it." Then I
hiked down the cliff goofing inside as I imagined the jogger telling
someone on the street about all of the bamboo washed in from Japan.

I'd been walking this stretch below the cliffs last spring when I
saw Sunday picnickers plodding toward me carrying enormous
whale ribs. The ribs rested in big arcs over their shoulders. Near
the point, I passed a man with a fin bone under his arm and another with a section of spine. A whale must have washed up on the
point, I thought, and I wanted to find a piece of it and take it
home, too. Before I reached the point, I passed a family bearing
various skeleton parts over their heads. I looked back at the column
of people receding between the cliff and the ocean; they looked like
worker ants hauling off a wishbone and the last bits of a turkey dinner.
At the place where the whale washed in, I found only footprints
surrounding an enormous pelvic bone too heavy to lift. I sat on it
for a while, watching the waves come in and an afternoon breeze
pushing at the green water.

"DID YOU WORK in the hardware store yesterday?" Miles asked during a lull. We floated in water leaping with flashes of sunlight. Cobalt blue waves emerged just inside the kelp bed, moving in like elephants, slow and single file.

"I worked the morning shift."

Two hours earlier, I'd thrown on my wetsuit and hiked down an empty beach. I waded into the tidal flat that runs out 20 yards or so before the water becomes deep enough to paddle in. I stepped gently, using my surfboard's buoyancy for balance. Knee-high sea grass moved languidly with the changing tide.

A red and white kelp cutter crossed the horizon. Enormous ships with open hungry bows, the cutters ingest kelp by the ton like giant masticating carp. This ship's deck was piled high with green matter. It looked gluttonous. After a cutter comes through, a mire of kelp refuse will eventually float into the break and end up lumped on the beach. A day or so later, it starts to rot. The smell is exactly what you might imagine a dead, rotting walrus to smell like—a fetid, organic musk.

Miles paddled out about an hour after I did. "So, you didn't see the cops up in the parking lot and all over the cliffs yesterday. It was crazy. They were making a sweep of the area."

"No," I said, "but I read something about it in the paper."

"Yeah," he said, "they were all over the cliff and down on the beach."

The morning newspaper revealed what everyone must have been thinking: "Police assigned a homicide team yesterday to investigate the death of Samantha Rae after anonymous callers contended that her death was a result of foul play, not a shark attack."

Miles remained convinced she'd been murdered. "They never found her clothes. She was completely naked when they pulled her out of the drink, you know. They didn't find her shoes," he said. "The purse, it was found on the beach. But there were no footprints around it. I bet some psycho lured her down here and broke her neck."

A wave popped up. Miles spun to catch it, paddling, but couldn't get in. He turned back to face me, sitting upright on his board.

"You bought brushes from her," I said. Somehow, my words came out like a sideways glance, an accusation. Miles focused on the kelp bed outside.

"What?"

"She worked at the art store. You bought brushes and watercolors from her. The girl with the red hair and the sleepy eyes—you said you wanted to paint her."

"I never," he said, shaking his head slowly.

A set bulged out of the horizon. I paddled out and into the peak, dropping into the first wave, too deep. I raced it awkwardly, backside, trying to make the shoulder. A wall of foam knocked the board from under me. Icy water rushed in through the neckline of my wetsuit. When I came up, my board had disappeared.

Miles laughed as I looked around, my head poking out of the water like a seal's. I swam toward the beach to a place where water pushed in, away from the channel. Lost boards almost always found their way there. When I reached the warmer water of the tidal flat, I stood and found my board rocking lightly in calm water.

Directly in front of me, like a lighthouse under the water, something sparkled in the sand between swaths of waving sea grass. A tiny wave moved through to the shore. The sea grass swayed with it, and the thing glimmered again. I separated the sea grass with my hand and grabbed it. It was a plastic case containing a yellow and white disposable camera, one of those waterproof jobs. I held it up and looked through the plastic lens out to sea. A glistening ocean, a pulsing swell and a horizon so flat and wide, if I could have walked on water then, I would have skipped right out to the break. I looked out there, then at the camera. An eight showed on the exposure dial. I wedged the plastic case into the sleeve of my suit and paddled back out to finish off the camera's shots on Miles' surfing.

IT WAS IN the hardware store, among the nuts and bolts and 16-penny nails that I'd first seen Samantha Rae. She'd walked past the window front on her way to the art store. I stood inches from the big window and watched as she glided past. Red hair to the middle of her back, pale legs and a brisk gait; she was not from this town. I could tell she didn't care about the yellowtail run offshore or the big swell coming from the south. She worked the afternoons and ate Chinese at the place across the street. She always carried a book or a magazine, and her nails were polished and clear. She never wore makeup. Didn't need to. The freckles on the bridge of her nose weren't sun marks, they were golden dabs of color.

Looking out from this same window, scrutinizing the world outside, I could see nothing had changed. Four days after Samantha was discovered at sea, and the thought of her death bubbled inside my gut like hot wax.

"You registered with the selective service?" my boss, Charlie, yelled from his office in the back of the store. He sat in there most afternoons reading the paper and cursing the events. Charlie would rest his feet on the desk and lean back in his chair, a newspaper stretched across his belly. A portrait of MacArthur hung above the slender door. "You better be registered," he said. "There's gonna be a draft."

Imminent drafts had their way with Charlie's imagination. He waved a large forearm at me from the office door. "Somebody's got to teach that Sadamn Hu-sane a lesson." He shook the newspaper. "There's a new shipment of molding out back. Stack it up front. Better get registered," he said.

I brought the wood molding in through dark aisles of fixtures, putties, tape and nails, and placed it in its vertical stacks. The place radiated the scent of decomposing industrial compounds. I could hear Charlie's chair wobbling on the linoleum. Then he shouted from his office: "You know the girl what was found dead in the ocean?"

"No," I yelled back.

I had asked her for the time three months before. It was a winter afternoon. I stepped onto the sidewalk outside the hardware store, and Samantha was there suspended before me. She wore a light green skirt and a sweater, red hair tousled about her shoulders. She stopped and looked me over with heavily lidded eyes. The sidewalk shuddered, I felt a distant quaking in my feet.

"What's wrong with the watch on your wrist," she said. My lips cracked a wane smile. I looked down at my arm.

"Broken," I said.

"Hmpf." She looked me over again and turned on a heel.

"Paper says she was your age," Charlie continued.

He was reading the last article the newspaper would print of Samantha Rae's death. Two paragraphs long, it was under the "Local News" heading on the eighth page. "Police homicide detectives said they have closed their investigation into the death of Samantha Rae, 24, because they are certain she was the victim of a shark attack, not murder. Detectives still cannot account for Rae's final hours."

From the window, I could see the Chinese place, a bookstore and a bike shop. I gazed out apprehensively when Charlie shouted again. "He said she was pretty in the face, despite the fact."

"Who?" I asked. It was like talking to a speaker phone.

"George was in here for some wire—the lobster fisherman what found the girl. Said that girl was chewed up real good. Said her leg was missin' almost up to the pelvis, the leg meat hanging out. I asked him if he thought the girl had been done in. He didn't know why, if it'd been a shark, why a shark wouldn't finish her off—just leave the body floating like that. I told 'em, 'George, that's the way sharks do, you know. They just take bites until they realize that you're a person.' Sharks don't like to eat people."

During World War II, Charlie had been an enlisted man in the Pacific Theater, a crew member on a gunner boat. He'd raced up and down an area near the Philippines known as "The Slot." He told me of battling the Japanese, of soldier's bodies floating like logs in the pale blue water and, by battle's end, of an ocean bubbling with the swarming of sharks. I thought he was going to go into it again, the telling of a horizon spotted by the bodies of floating soldiers. He didn't. But my stomach turned anyway.

On Wednesdays inland farmers fill the main drag with their tarps and stands of oranges, melons, squash, apples, peaches and whatnot. The street is closed to traffic. A local woman brings llamas she raises in her yard and charges kids 50 cents a ride. The llamas amble along the street like walking carpets, dropping marble-sized turds. Hippies on the sidewalk hammer their acoustic guitars and tambourines. On my way to the camera store, I passed a couple of them chortling a Neil Young tune, something about a summer sun. I paid for the photos with quarters from the hardware store's candy machine and stepped outside. An afternoon sun angled down on the street meekly, raking across the colored tarps.

Despite the noise and color of the farmer's market, the hardware store remained as dark and as quiet as a library. Charlie was still reading the paper when I returned. He called out my name.

"Yeah," I said. "What?"

But I didn't want to know what. No, Charlie, I don't want to hear about World War II, George the lobster fisherman, Samantha or the selective service. No more history. No more current events. I didn't want to think any longer about human bodies and water. No cement shoes, no drowned fishermen, no storm flood victims, not Esteban, not Ahab, not Jonah. I no longer wanted the power of the dead to return by water in this life. I wanted the circles to become lines; I wanted the tides to become rivers—here now and gone tomorrow and forever. No more of the living returning with the dead, the way George had come bobbing into the harbor with Samantha's body on deck, piled like so many lobster traps.

This is the reason why: when I opened the photo envelope that day and flipped through the shots I'd taken of Miles surfing on a sunny blue-sky afternoon, I never expected a sense of music, or an image of Samantha.

Doc, a character from Steinbeck's *Cannery Row*, found a young girl wedged between rocks, partly covered by moss just below the ocean's surface. As a biologist, he'd been collecting baby octopuses from a reef not far from here. The story was set in the '40s, and I suppose the reef must have jumped with life then. Moss beneath the surface swayed in the tide, and he saw the girl's pale, rested face. Something I thought about when I read the book but not much since then was the flute music Doc heard at the time. A music born of disquiet. Steinbeck described an eternally serene melody, something you'd never hear in nature not on the ocean, not in the tide pools. A sense of that tune came to me, though, when I flipped through the shots of Mile's surfing and instead laid my eyes on the first of eight photos of Samantha Rae.

I recognized the sandstone cliffs immediately. The girl in that first photo is smiling; yes, it's Samantha, and she's smiling. The ocean at her back, a light wind pulling at her long red hair. She's holding a blouse in her right hand. Her breasts are pale, peppered with freckles, and her nipples are small and erect. A skirt band crosses just below her navel, her pale abdomen rising out of it and into her full chest, slight shoulders and a neck lightly tanned. She faces the camera at an angle, the smile genuine and eyes somewhat distrustful, like an intimate touch on a first date. It's obvious that she is holding the camera out before herself. She is alone on the beach and undressing. She looks proud—chin up, chest out, knees slightly turned in. The following photos reveal her nude body and bashful poses, glances of daring.

It wasn't until I saw the photo of her clothes piled on the beach just below the high-water mark, that I understood. This was Samantha's proof. For a lover, maybe, for her family back home or maybe her friends and now me. This was her documented evidence. She could swim naked, alone, in the vast ocean on a gray afternoon and return. Samantha wasn't afraid.

El Brazo

ROCKING LIKE AN idiot savant seemed to ease the pain. I sat on a bench outside a thatch *cabaña*. I cradled my right arm and rocked. The arm swelled, visibly, from what must have been 50 mosquito bites. I'd laughed the night before while crawling under a girlishly yellow mosquito net—this netting draped over a bed of horse blankets looking as though it was prepared for a native princess. Wads of tissue paper were stuffed haphazardly between tears in the netting. The white puffs floated above me like plankton caught in a drift net. I felt silly and impish lying under it.

But in my sleep, my right arm fell against the netting, and the invisible mosquitoes descended, tapping my flesh through the weave. The swelling woke me just before sunrise—the arm rippled with punctures from elbow to pinkie. It pulsated. The skin grew taut, a 10-pound package in a five-pound bag.

An indignant rooster cackled as the sun rose, and the smell of ineffective mosquito repellent gave way to a daytime odor of trash fires. This trash-fire ambrosia engulfed the smell of ocean salt and the musk of a far-off jungle. As the sun slid up over the mountains to the east, the odor expanded like a low-lying fog.

It's obscene now to think it, but before my first morning in Ecuador, I anticipated a broad swath of artificial color extending east to west over the horizon—a tangible line marking the equator. It would be translucent and hovering, an atmospheric hue of color, the visible barrier between north and south. I expected jungles, too—what explorers called the "green death." I expected toucans and monkeys.

But there was no jungle to speak of and nothing to divide hemispheres. The morning light broadened, revealing a ramshackle oceanfront ranch. My first morning in Ecuador was this ranch, a scrawny red rooster, a few hens, a white swaybacked horse, the smell of trash fires and Carlito.

I'd gathered that Carlito was the ranch lackey. He'd been sweeping dirt between the *cabañas* just before dawn. He was a small boy with a dark bowl cut and heavy eyes. He swept the dirt. He moved brick blocks from one spot and stacked them in another. Dirty white hens pecked around his ankles. Through gapped teeth, he clucked at them. I didn't think much of the dirty-faced boy. At least not until later, when I watched him get pummeled by five big redheaded boys.

Outside the *cabaña* I rocked ever so slightly and listened to the ocean not a hundred yards away. My mind mingled with worst-case scenarios. I'd seen this mural from a bus window the day before. A stick man is bitten by a giant mosquito. Through enormous fangs, the giant mosquito injects parasites into the stick man. The stick man becomes ill, goes to the hospital and dies. "Muerto", the mural said. Dead.

My image of Ecuador became more crooked as this place before me became more beautiful. I tried to remember the word for hospital and the word for emergency. Carlito appeared in the dirt drive. He raked at rocks now. The white horse guffawed. The very tips of the trees shuddered at the growing offshore breeze.

They must have been lying in wait, these five redheaded boys. Because I looked away briefly and back again, and they had strategically surrounded Carlito in the dirt drive. Their collective body language suggested a real sack-o-rocks beating. I couldn't hear what they were saying, but I could see the look on Carlito's face. Unbelievably, he looked listless. The biggest boy smacked him on the head. The others taunted and poked him. They kicked at the dirt he'd been sweeping. One punched him in the back.

The white horse, which had been standing nearby all morning, swatted flies with its tail. The red rooster cackled in spurts.

Suddenly, the pack of boys became a monster of knees and elbows, a cactus with five red heads and a dark center. I stood and yelled: "Hey, you little cocksuckers!" They didn't so much as look over. "Why don't you piranhas beat it," I yelled again. The biggest redhead then looked at me blankly. He had this fat, indifferent face. Closer, I could see that the redheaded boys weren't all the same size, but that each was a progressively shorter version of the same boy. *Hermanos.* All with the same indignant pie face, brown eyes and spiky red hair.

The biggest boy surveyed Carlito bent over in the dirt. He

bracketed his left leg for a good strong boot to the ribs. My legs picked up speed and I started running at them. I raised my speckled lobster claw of a right arm and yelled, "Awww!" like a hungry Chupa Cabra. I yelled, "Awww!" and felt a warm delight in their dirty-faced, snot-nosed terror. Like hoofed animals, the boys scrambled for a sense of direction. But as I came upon them, they bolted in a group—including Carlito, a brown dot amid the redheaded pack, running away toward the road.

WAITING FOR SET waves, I wondered if I was surfing on the equator yet or if I was still south of it. The green ocean water felt great on my arm. The green darkened to blue farther out. I imagined that the darker water marked the Humboldt current, pulsing by on its way to Alaska.

A tan rock face above the beach broke into talus and stumbled into the ocean, creating this almost perfect right point. The waves were small but fun, and they peeled all the way to the beach. The sun began to set over the Pacific, but this green ocean water seemed to retain its brilliance. At dusk, the white ocean foam took on a phosphorescent glow.

Walking in from the beach, I noticed Carlito playing among weathered fishing boats. I was still wet, and I carried my board. When I caught his eye, I raised my fat arm and yelled, "Awww!" It was becoming dark, and I saw the whites of his eyes flare briefly. Then he laughed. He held his hand up and rolled his fingers into a fist, like a wave crashing. "*Olas*," he said.

"*Sí*," I said.

Before reaching Ecuador, I'd been traveling by bus along the desert coast of northern Peru. I stayed in fishing villages and combed the coast for waves. Sweeping left-hand points line that stretch of desert, jutting into the Humboldt current, sun-bleached and spare, arched like the ridges of an iguana. The points have names like Punta Blanca and Chicama. But, for me, the waves never grew more than waist-high. Waiting, leering at the ocean like an expatriate, I became the worst kind of traveler: an impatient one. I traveled from place to place faster, probably, than a traveler should.

I arrived at the coast of Ecuador around midnight. The bus driver called for the passengers to tell the *norte americano* to get off the bus. Lights shot from a two-story log-and-rock *casa* 50 yards from the road. Leaving me there, the *salsa* bus sputtered off down the blackened road. A door in the *casa* squealed open, and seconds later, a man appeared from the darkness, walking toward the gate. "My friend," the man called out, "I am Rodrigo, *el diablo loco*." He laughed, hacking. When he ambled close enough, I could see his wry grin and bloodshot eyes. Tufts of hair ringed his scalp and bangs, looking as though he'd been in some kind of fishing accident. The smell of booze hung on him like smoke. "You want a room?" he asked. He opened the gate and led me to a small *cabaña*. Inside this *cabaña*, I saw the girlish, yellow mosquito net draped over a bed of horse blankets.

THE ROOSTER ANNOUNCED dawn the next morning with an alarming staccato squawk, as though the rooster were grappling with death. For a time, I thought some jungle animal had crawled out of the hills for an easy slaughter. I would have been glad for it, too, the permanent silencing of that arrogant rooster. But the cackling continued long after the rooster should have been finished by its predator.

I opened the *cabaña* door to see a ranch that sparkled green and brown, the blue smoke of trash fires in the distance, and behind them a range of foreboding jungle hills. The rooster now plucked along happily, his harem of white hens scattered about the ranch.

Walking down a sandy path, past beached fishing boats, I heard pounding surf before I could see the water. I knew there'd been a change before I got a decent view of the point. The waves had grown well overhead, and the swell stacked up in emerald lines. As the waves stood, their color lightened. The faces broke first off the endmost rocks of the point. The shoulders whipped past like tails uncoiling. Molecules of seawater burst skyward from the impact. The sound of thunderous crashing refracted from the point's tan rock face.

My arm was still plump, and the mosquito bites had defined themselves like atolls rising up out of sore flesh. I didn't feel feverish then, and there was nothing, I thought, that could be done for it anyway. I grabbed my board and paddled out.

Sometime later, after returning from the beach, I saw Rodrigo stumble out of his *casa* looking more downtrodden than his sway-backed horse. The hair ringing his head shot out on one side like a broken wing. It hit me that his mottled hair resembled a faded red, just as the five redheaded boys trampled out of the *casa*. Wearing backpacks, they piled into Rodrigo's diesel 4x4. Rodrigo worked some magic trick under the hood; it started with a sputter. He climbed in and the whole gaggled clambered away.

Twenty minutes passed before the 4x4 returned, pulling along a tail of blue exhaust. The vehicle humped into the dirt drive. It stalled and coasted to a halt near the *casa*. I heard the door slam, and then a moment of silence. I looked over to see this scabby Chihuahua of a man scampering toward me. He screamed some words I couldn't understand. His boozy breath preceded him. He stopped 3 feet before me, slapping his bare chest. "*Mis niños,*" he said. Rodrigo's eyes bulged, and the fierce veins in them were carameled over by a thick film. His babble gave way to a violent wheezing. From the only words I understood, "my boys," I realized he must not have liked my haranguing his little bullies with my swollen club arm. I had no idea, at that point, what his violent redheads had told him. I played utterly dumb. There seemed nothing else to say.

Then he looked at my right arm, not with disgust, but with a kind of loathsome introspection. His wheezing slowed. He put his hands on his hips, looked skyward, then at my arm again. He pointed at the open door of my *cabaña*. "*Tres mil*," he said solemnly—three thousand Ecuadorian, which rounds out roughly to $3, the price of his *cabañas* per night.

"*Sí*," I said. He nodded slowly. I suspected Rodrigo was going to raise my rent, some sort of haranguer's tax. But then, he said simply, "*Tus pasaporte*." He wanted my passport, a measure pensioners sometimes take to secure a tenant's rent. I'd sooner have eaten a light bulb salad than give this scabby man my passport. I played dumb. "*No comprendo*," I said. He tried to explain the necessity of his holding my passport. "*No sé*," I said. He shook his head and gave up.

Carlito came pedaling along the dirt drive on a small bike. He wore a backpack. As he passed, Rodrigo told him to hurry and tried to smack him on the back of the head. Carlito ducked and continued out to the road. "*¿Dónde vas?*" I called after him.

"*Escuela*," he answered cheerily. School.

Carlito returned 30 minutes later. I almost asked, "What has happened?" Did he forget something? But then I realized he no longer carried the backpack. Carlito's trip to school was an errand, the delivery of the backpack to one of Rodrigo's forgetful sons. My heart sank a bit when, heading out for a surf that afternoon, I noticed Carlito sweeping the dirt outside a vacant *cabaña*.

THE SWELLING ABATED, and my arm reduced to an almost nor-
mal shape. Still, by the third day, I knew something was terribly
wrong. Like low tide revealing boulders, the decreased swelling
revealed knots anchored below the surface flesh. The knots took on
the round firmness of boils. They were reddened and ripe looking.
All of which supported my decision.

It was the thought of a pretty girl that compelled my decision to
leave the coast and seek medical attention. The girl, whom I'd met
on a bus out of Trijillo, was an Australian. I noticed the scar on her
cheek right off the bat. It was pinkishly fresh, still in the process of
healing. She told me she'd been in Argentina when a small bump
developed on her cheek. The bump grew into a boil, then grew
some more, and finally she went to see a doctor. The doctor lanced
the boil with a scalpel, revealing a sack of worms; each worm the
diameter of a pencil eraser.

The surf had grown even larger than it had the day before. And
the shape only improved with size. Most surprising, though, were
the five surfers floating in the lineup. Once I'd paddled out, I
noticed four of the surfers rode these obese boards shaped from
native balsa wood and embalmed with an impenetrable layer of
fiberglass. One surfer rode a newish foam board. He looked
younger than the balsa crew, dropped in deeper and stalled at precise moments. When he dropped into a set wave and then blew a
stylish fan out the back, one of his *compadres* paddled up to me and
said stoically, "He is Ricardo, the best surfer in all of Ecuador."

They cheered him on, chanting "Ricardo," as though he were a famous matador.

Sets piled in consistently, until the six of us were strewn along the break. When one surfer charged a section, the rest would yell, "*Chucha*!" Fuck! When one of us fell, they would yell, "*Chucha*!" again. It was some of the best surf of our lives, and we were all "*Chuchadores*." When I dropped into the one wave I remember even now, and its green skin began to fold over me, I heard warbled voices from the shoulder say, "*El Brazo*," and then, "*Chucha*!" And I was elated, until I realized the surfers were calling me "The Arm."

I emerged from the water drained. I walked past the beached fishing boats, toward the *cabañas*. In the surf, I'd concentrated on not looking at my arm. It was wrinkled the way fresh water can wrinkle your fingertips. The boils looked more resolute and eternal. I walked down this ranch trail next to the ocean. It gleamed with an absolute beauty, and fear invaded me like subtle fever.

At the *cabaña* I pulled all of my belongings outside and packed in the sun. I found a long-sleeve shirt and buttoned the sleeve over my riddled arm, rolling up the sleeve on the other. The swaybacked horse milled about some weeds at the edge of the dirt drive. The rooster stood idle while his harem of hens pecked at the dirt. Carlito walked into the drive with his broom. And I hoped to the bottom of my heart that he wouldn't start sweeping the dirt. "*¿Mas grande, no?*" he shouted. "*Las olas.*"

"*Sí. Mucho!*" I answered. He smiled through gapped teeth.

"*Sí, grande,*" he said. I looked down at my packing and knew that I needed to find a gift for Carlito. I had some red tape and a slim pocket knife. There was also the compass, my watch and a couple American dollars. These are no good, I thought. Peering over my shoulder I saw Carlito sweeping at the dirt, and then I saw my surfboard where I'd set it to dry.

"Carlito," I yelled, "come quickly." He walked over cautiously, clutching his broom. I picked up the board and held it out: "*Un regalo,*" I said. A gift. He looked frightened. "*Un regalo,*" I insisted, shaking the board. Carlito stooped and gently set down his broom. He took the surfboard, wrapping his arms around it.

"*Gracias,*" he said and tried to smile by showing his gapped teeth. His eyelids lifted, and his lips stretched. He stepped back and turned to hurry away while attempting to keep his eyes on me. "*Gracias,*" he said again over his shoulder.

Rodrigo must have seen me packing. He opened the *casa* door, looked across the yard and said in Spanish, "Carlito, what are you doing with that?"

"*El Brazo,*" he said. "The Arm gave it to me."

Rodrigo shut the door. I could hear some stumbling about inside. He opened it again and scampered over to my *cabaña*. "Where are you going?" he asked.

"North," I said, still packing. "Maybe to Quito." He stood with his hands on his hips, surveying the things I was stuffing into my bag.

"To see a doctor?" he asked. I looked up at him. It was noon, and he'd obviously just gotten out of bed. His eyes were bloodshot and his skin shined.

"Do you know of one around here?" I asked.

"No."

"Then, I'm going. What do I owe you?" I settled with Rodrigo. He seemed too lethargic to count the bills I'd handed him.

Then he asked, "Do you have any gifts for my kids?"

"No," I said.

"Goodbye," he said, turning toward the *casa* and waving the money. Carlito had disappeared.

I walked down the dirt drive and out to the road. The hills far beyond rose from green pastures to elevations of blue. I waited for the once-a-day bus. I wondered how long it would be before I crossed the equator. I wondered if, when the time came, I would know the words to answer a doctor's questions. Something I thought I knew for certain: there could be no better gift for a boy who lived on a perfect right point than a surfboard. And I hoped surfers out at the point would someday be saying, "He is Carlito, the best surfer in all of Ecuador." I thought about small miracles.

The bus came humping down the road on tired shocks, painted like a candy store. I stepped on board with only my pack. Salsa music sputtered from blown out speakers. I found a window seat facing the ranch. It was bright and green and brown. Then I saw Carlito in the drive again, holding his new board. And, I admit, I

was proud for a brief moment. The bus began to pull away. I
started to wave. Then I noticed the five redheads. They quickly
surrounded Carlito. He clutched the surfboard desperately. The
bus ground gears and gasped. And I wondered, painfully, if
what I'd just given Carlito wasn't a surfboard at all, but only
another beating.

Sketches of the East

"DON'T SWALLOW THE water. It's full of pig shit."

A drawl interrupted my quiet surf just a short distance from North Carolina's famous Cape Hatteras lighthouse. We sat on our boards in water thick with sediment. At least I thought it was sediment coloring the water a fine milky brown. I hadn't been talking to the other guy out and thought it was enough just to enjoy the afternoon surf. Maybe he'd seen me take a gulp of the brown water. I couldn't remember. I didn't really look at him until that warning, and when I did, it was obvious that the man knew what he was talking about. Even in his wetsuit, he looked like a pig farmer. He wore a thick beard and let his mouth gape, revealing chipped, yellow teeth. I'd later learn that he was right, in a sense. Waterways on the other side of this overgrown sandbar all the way to the interior of North Carolina were full of pig shit. The last hurricane to come through here leveled North Carolina's interior, flooded its abundant pig farms and sent overflowing hog ponds, drowned pigs and septic tank discharge down river into the ocean.

Ominously, 6-foot lines formed in brown stacked up along the beach. We surfed next to a metal girder that didn't look like it would feel too nice if you botched the drop and landed on it. Down the beach, closer to the lighthouse, a gaggle of young contenders in the Eastern Surfing Association championships vied for position outside another girder. From where we sat, the pandemonium looked like a flea circus gone to the beach. I'd actually walked up here to escape them, but the surfing pig farmer said as a way of introduction, "You here for the contest?"

"Nope," I said.

"Good for you." After a wave rolled through, he added, "These boys ain't gonna have their contest tomara'. There's gonna be 25 mph north, northwest winds and an 8- to 10-foot swell."

The next day, I'd wake to discover the Hatteras prophet's prediction spot on, which only served to reinforce my suspicion that listening to Easterners was just as important as being here.

FROM THE SURF media, an American can learn more about the surf zones surrounding the distant Indian Ocean than about the largest seaboard of our own country. Annual editorials on hurricane season do little to fill in the picture and appear, seemingly, only to satiate one of the surf industry's largest markets. Considering that the East Coast has given us dynamic world champions, some of our best freesurfers and a good chunk of America's brightest stars on the World Championship Tour today, the neglect is more than happenstance. The absence of the East Coast in surf media has been so thorough that the East doesn't even hold an archetype with which to battle. California surfing has yet to shirk off the cultural monikers given to it by Malibu and Gidget and early Hollywood.

Modern Hawaiian surfing still revels in the kitsch of its Waikiki roots. But surfing on the East Coast is...what?

For the surf media gatekeepers of Southern California to send out a foreign journalist, as though cultural and language barriers had prevented any crossing of the divide before, didn't feel quite right either. But there I was—rental car, surfboard and a small list of contacts—a hired gun. Still, I told myself, sometimes the best way to get a fresh perspective of a place is to go in blind and hungry, like a teenage runaway. Maybe I would learn something the hard way.

AT THIS TRIP'S outset, in the surf of Florida's Sebastian Inlet, I found myself watching a large gray, fleshy thing rising out of the waves. It came up as effortlessly as a bubble. Its movement wasn't the muscled oscillation of a shark—so I relaxed a bit. Maybe the creature was dead. It certainly lulled about like a dead thing—an apparent corpse dislodged from the depths. But then, as it descended and rose again, it showed signs of self-mobility. Maybe it was wounded, this something-or-other.

There are only about 1,300 manatees left in these waters, and coming from the West Coast, I never expected to be surfing with a sea cow—an apparition as likely to me as Puff the Magic Dragon. Maybe I should have been prepared for even Puff, every living thing seemed to be joining us in the water. It simmered with baby mullet so abundant that the school forced swirls and patterns onto the surface like the brushwork of Van Gogh's "Starry Night." The tails of blue fish smacked the surface as they lit after and swallowed the young mullet. Other fish jumped and skipped out of the ocean as though it would be nothing but a thing to flap their fins into the sky and migrate south for the coming winter. Likely, the fish would have flown into the maws of the pelicans and smaller birds going absolutely berserk above us, climbing, climbing, climbing, and diving beak first into the sea. Thwack!

Then a random porpoise breached with a huff, flipped its tail and took off.

High and dry on the jetty, sun-battered fishermen cast their lines with the mad perseverance of gamblers at slot machines.

Still, what I didn't see, but knew to be lurking below, were the sharks. There are heaps of sharks in Florida's waters, mostly small ones, but they're mean little fuckers. As a result, there are more shark attacks here than anywhere in the United States. Stories abound of lacerated toes and feet as sharks mistakenly take surfer's parts for wounded fish. In 2001 there was a boy in Pensacola who nearly lost an arm to a bigger shark. His uncle caught it on a line and attempted to reel the fish into shore where the boy waited for it. The shark did, in fact, sever the arm from the boy's body. But the uncle wrestled the shark onto the beach. A ranger's bullet finally ended the shark's fight, and medical personnel quickly cut it open to retrieve the arm. At a nearby hospital, the arm was eventually repatriated to the boy, and he wears it still. The uncle and his nephew seemed to be good examples of the people here—sun-baked and tough.

This day, among the manatee and other creatures, was damn near perfect, I thought; sand dunes strewn with palmetto brush, the sky only shades bluer than the warm sea, tropical clouds marching with the idle girth of elephants, the haywire birds, the porpoise and a humdinger of a mullet run. But there was a weighty feeling behind it. We were frolicking in the heart of hurricane season. The biggest hurricane in decades had just nearly come ashore here. Every home along this stretch between the Indian River and the coast had been forcibly evacuated. Bridges to the mainland had been closed. Two days after the storm, one in 10 homes was without power. Flotsam from washed out condos still peppered the beach and the water. That day in the water, the feeling among the surfers seemed to me like that of an Eskimo village emerging to glean what it could from a fair weather day between snowstorms. Another hurricane was just around the corner.

I LEFT MELBOURNE Beach just as the first bands of rain from the new hurricane breached land. My idea was to make the Outer Banks of North Carolina to meet it and then head farther to New England. It's a classic trip for East Coasters. As hurricanes project northward, the only option is to follow them.

Maps are deceiving; I thought it would be an easy drive. But what I didn't know was that the East Coast is much longer than the

West Coast, and my finger measurements of actual distance failed me. At least I was able to see it: that Bermuda Triangle of American culture known as Florida. Palms gave way to pines on Highway 95. After seeing a Camaro parked beside trailers in the pines, I turned the radio dial to a classic rock station. If it had been Miami, maybe a Cuban station, but Central Florida, definitely classic rock. Sprouting here and there signs of Californication appeared, stucco strip malls among the spindly pines. It's an odd combination: palmettos, pines, trailer parks and stucco. But Florida is a combination of the weird, the site of the fountain of youth and our largest retirement communities, rednecks and fashion idols, skyscrapers and swampland, conspiracy theory and apathy, mangrove and Disney World. As I passed the turnoff to America's oldest town, St. Augustine, I saw hulking advertisements reading: "Food 'N' Fun, Topless Café" or "Next Exit: 13 foot Gator!"

The sun began to set and I found myself careening over meandering Georgia wetlands. The golden light brought the bending rivulets into silvery serpents and lent the surrounding grass a golden color that seemed to hum in the light. Bunches of leafy trees broke one wetland from another, but looking down their course, they seemed to extend forever. When the light finally died, I found a turnoff and took it to a standard of the South, the Waffle House. A man sitting at the counter inside, wearing a camouflage trucker hat, a thick mustache and no front teeth, asked me, "What in the hell you got on the roof, boy?"

We looked outside through the big windows where, apparently, I'd parked my rental next to his truck. I looked at the roof of my rental, then at the two dead dear draped on his truck's cab. I turned to the toothless man and said, "That would have to be surf-boards, son."

I WOULD ARRIVE at the Outer Banks knowing only slightly more about the area than the original English settlers did in 1585. But then, this group up and split back to England within a year. The next group established their colony at Roanoke in 1587, yet disappeared from the face of the earth within three years. What happened to them is a mystery still. The only evidence the settlers left behind was the word "Croatan" carved into a tree. Some say the word refers to a place, other say it refers to an Indian tribe that wiped the colony out.

Driving along Highway 12 past endless waterways, marshes and what seemed to be the largest sandbar in the world, I thought about the "Lost Colony," about Blackbeard—the famed pirate who plied these waters—and about the innumerable ships to run aground here over the past four hundred years. There's a feeling that something resides beneath these sand dunes glimmering in the hot wind, yet maybe it's just the feeling of history.

I'd later meet a surfer named Chris who'd been living on the Outer Banks for about a year. He'd come by way of the Bahamas. Ambiguously, he said that he thought there was something suspicious going on here. "What, for example?" I asked.

"I'm not sure," he said, casting a weary eye on the surf.

"Something. But it's an island, and you know what they say about islands: 'Sunny places for shady people.'"

More like tough places for tough people, I thought. But the two ambiguous feelings could be easily confused.

The contest at the lighthouse resumed a day after the winds eased. Mobs of young surfers diverged on the area. So I drove south looking for another sandbar. Where, exactly, I had no idea. Driving through a wooded area I spotted two boys hitchhiking with surfboards. I pulled over and opened the trunk. They looked about 13 years old, one blond, one brown-haired. They each carried a 5-foot-nothing surfboard and a backpack. Stacking their midget surfboards on top of mine, the blond kid asked, "Hey, you goin' surfin', mister?"

"Yep," I said.

"Where?"

"Wherever you are," I said. The two boys looked at each other.

"You ain't from around here, are ya?" the brown-haired boy asked.

Once on our way, the boys said that they'd been getting good surf that season, but that the tidal surge during the last hurricane had washed out roads and "kids had to be taken to school in big trucks, like that one."

The blond pointed at a massive National Guard truck parked along the road. I'd read about that particular tidal surge. It had covered parts of the island in 13 feet of water. It had loosened ancient graves on Ocracoke Island until caskets seeped up out of the mud and floated away.

The brown-haired boy pointed to something else along the road, "Hey, look et the dead deer!"

As we passed the carrion, the blond added, "That was a big 'un."

I asked why they weren't competing in the contest. They let a moment pass. "Aw, well, 'cause we just wanna go surfin'," the brown-haired boy said finally.

Since I was going surfing with them—had, in fact, invited myself on their surf trip—they asked me to pull over at a mom-and-pop hamburger joint on the way. They ran in and came out with armloads of wrapped hot dogs and hush puppies. We turned down a sandy road and parked and hiked over a dune with our boards, hotdogs and hush puppies. A hot wind blew offshore, grooming 2- to 3-foot peaks up and down the beach. The only other humans along that stretch were a few scattered fishermen who'd made camp next to their 4x4s. I couldn't say why we'd come here of all places: it looked like every other sandbar on the island. Yet we hadn't been out in the warm water and small waves more than 20 minutes before another crew of boys turned up.

Now, the boys I'd taken to the beach were from Hatteras. The new arrivals were from Avon, which I'd learn was good reason to start yelling at them. "You don't belong here," the blond yelled. "Go back to Avon, fat ass!"

The other kids yelled back, and insults were returned. When the disses subsided a bit—and I'd stopped laughing—I asked why they didn't like the kids from Avon. The blond said, "'Cause they're inbred."

"'Cause they're kooks," the brown-haired boy added.

Seeing as how the two towns are separated only by a couple of miles of sand and vacation homes, I pressed the boys on what, exactly, was the reason for the feud. "'Cause nobody likes 'em," the blond said matter-of-factly.

But I only had to wait a little while and catch a few more tiny waves before I discovered that all of the boys knew each other on a first-name basis; that the insults and name-calling were just a formality that had to be completed; and that all of them surfed here and insulted each other just about every time the wind blew this direction.

I was pretty amazed at how the boys were able to pull into the tiny barrels coming through. The best I could do was floaters over them, but even that became boring, so I went in and just watched. I was too big to get barrels out there and, maybe, too old to be hanging out with a bunch of 13 year olds. But I felt like I was experiencing something I hadn't in a long time. Pretty soon they all came in, began insulting each other again in a lighter way, sat down together and ate their cold hot dogs and hush puppies.

One of them finally asked where I was from. "Wow, California," he said. "The waves are good there, huh?"

But even as I shrugged and answered his question, I realized that I couldn't imagine a better place to be a grom than here: riding your bike or hitchhiking to an empty beach with your board, a bag of hush puppies, some friends to insult and an entire day to kill doing it.

"IF YOU'RE NOT writing a book about me already, you should be," said Sid Abruzzi. We were taking what he calls the "Package Tour," a unique look at the reefs and historical spots of Newport, Rhode Island, with its most outspoken surfer. Sid's nickname, by the way, is the "Package." When I asked how he'd come by it, Sid balked and waved his hand from the steering wheel, "Isn't it obvious?"

I shrugged. He frowned and offered as if to a nitwit, "It's all included in the Package." If you were of a certain age in Newport, the Package really did include everything. This was in 1998, on the tail end of a mammoth hurricane season that included Floyd and Gert. Sid, being at the height of his renown in New England, was not only the man to see there, but gracious enough to give journalistic drive-thrus like myself his personal tour. At the time, he was the co-owner of the local skate park and founder of the area's most well-known surf shop, Water Bros. But more than this, he served as patriarch and energetic spokesman for the local surf community. And he wasn't too shy to admit it.

We pulled into an empty beach parking lot, and Sid pointed to a little café, "That's where my punk band used to play."

Sid was in his 40s. When he mentioned the band, I asked, "You like punk?"

"Kid," he said in his oil-thick New England accent, "I started punk." As far as Newport, Rhode Island, goes, that may be true.

Fall trees blazed with color and shrouded the road in the flickering light of a stained glass window. The coast here is a jigsaw of rock outcroppings, inlets and islands connected by bridges. It's not an easily accessible coast. The roads didn't seem to have been planned but merely laid over centuries-old farm routes. A deep knowledge of the place is plain necessary to navigate them. Without Sid behind the wheel, I'd have been lost before I started.

Prior to laying eyes on Ruggles, the most notable reef in the area, I imagined parking on a road in the trees and hiking a dirt path to the ocean. I imagined a kind of New England ruggedness. The reality is shocking. The right and left peak sits at the back porches of some of the most stately mansions I'd ever seen. They'd been the summer homes to the likes of the Rockefellers and Astors. The environment reeked with their exclusivity. Parking wasn't allowed on the tree-lined streets, and Sid said there was a time when even surfing here was against the law. Sid himself had been arrested twice for the violation before a judge overturned the municipal code, partly because of Sid's protest. So, in Newport, he'd been a coastal rights activist, too.

Now there seemed to be an unofficial surfer's code in the shadow of these vacant-looking mansions. I noticed graffiti on a handrail overlooking the break that read, "No kooks and longboarders, please." I've seen graffiti like this all over the world, but it took a New Englander to add the proper "please."

Under the ivy-covered exclusivity lived an almost palpable history. "See that rock? That's called Hangman's Rock. That's because they used to hang pirates from it." Sid lifted one of his bushy eyebrows.

Wheeling his car through the turns, he also mentioned a much more famous rock nearby. "Plymouth Rock is about a mile away," he began. "Shit, you can surf Plymouth Rock. You can!"

We whipped in and out of the neighborhood backstreets until we found ourselves on a promontory overlooking a still slate of ocean. We parked in front of the area's most exclusive crab club. These people take their crabs seriously. If the club had been open, we'd have been kicked out of the parking lot already. Walking to the cliff's edge, Sid pointed out a bubbling in the water a couple of hundred yards out. What we were surveying, he said, was one of Newport's most coveted jewels, a barreling big-wave break. Then he made me promise not to mention the break's name, which I thought was senseless at the time. It broke once or twice a year, if that, and you'd have to be a climatologist to figure out when that was. Sid on the other hand, would know. He'd been keeping daily notes of Newport's conditions and the details of his sessions for years. The notebooks included the recent span covering hurricanes Floyd and Gert, between them there were a couple of 14-foot days. Doing the math, I realized I was just a few days short of seeing this

Halley's Comet of surf breaks come alive. Sid confirmed it.

"During a big swell, there's maybe 30 to 40 surf options: Narragansett, Newport, Little Compton, Jamestown." We were back in the car and on the way to check the last resort for waves that day, a sandbar.

But mostly, Sid continued, Newport surfers received what he called "24-hour specials." These swells would come up and fade in the breadth of a workday. "It's like we've got a cupcake mold here," Sid said. "We could make perfect cupcakes, but we've got no cupcake mix."

This conundrum and the harsh conditions of New England breed a dedicated surfer. "With work, it's suicide. My friends who are contractors won't hire the young surfers I know. If there's a good swell, the surfers will disappear, maybe for a week. The surfers know that if they miss it, there might not be swell for a long time."

Before we'd set out that day, Sid knew we wouldn't find anything surfable. He'd put an optimistic light on the situation for my benefit, as well as for the sake and continuity of the Package Tour. I realized this after we'd given up our wayward surf check and Sid wheeled naturally to the place he'd planned to end up all day: the pub next to his surf shop. This Package Tour, as I'm sure they all are, had been timed perfectly to end at happy hour, at the bar. This was fine with me. It proved to be as close an education into the New England surfing experience as possible without paddling into the frigid Atlantic.

As we ordered our first beers, the wood- and brass-trimmed pub began to fill with local surfers getting off their day jobs. They were twenty-something painters, carpenters and plumbers; guys who knew they could lose their jobs depending on the timing of the next swell to come into Newport's window, who remained here after the rich and famous had vacated their summer homes, who waited on pins and needles for the dog days of hurricane season and the winter swells that follow. Any outsider allowed to linger among them could tell, they were Sid's boys, as thick as the seafarers who'd historically made harbor here. Some eyed me wearily, some eventually confided local secrets. And after a few beers, I was tutored in lessons I never thought a Californian would learn in a bar: salt water freezes at 29 degrees, a surf session can actually be warmer when it's snowing, a little hypothermia is good for the body and it's best to drive to and from the surf session in wetsuit and gloves, leaving the key in the ignition as to avoid wrestling it with nearly frozen fingers.

I can't say that I've ever actually scored on the East Coast. I thought I'd surfed good waves on the Outer Banks, but a surfer who really knows the place, my friend Jason Borte, asked me, "Did you do any turns?"

"Yeah, I did plenty of turns," I said.

"Then you didn't get it good. When it's on, you don't do any turns. You just pull in."

I've been painfully close to scoring eastern perfection on several occasions. And I'm willing to take the blame for failing. Yet, hurricanes rip up the coast in a matter of days, they stall and advance, and like a couple of groms growing up on the Outer Banks, they do pretty much the same thing each time but are free to change that plan every time. The genius of the place, really, is a surf culture that isn't hampered down by 50 years of floral print mythology, a place where surfers are free to be as city or redneck or New England as they wanna be. And although I've traveled there as a tourist in my own country, have been mystified that one can actually surf at the base of Atlantic City or Plymouth Rock, can ride the subway to a surf session, I've felt a little more free each time I surf there, too.

Father Joe's Invitation

"KALAUPAPA NATIONAL HISTORICAL Park was established on December 22, 1980. Still in its formative years, it is dedicated to the past, the present and the future. It is dedicated to preserving the memories and experiences of the past in order that valuable lessons might be learned from them. It is dedicated to providing a well-maintained community to ensure that the present residents of the Settlement may live out their lives in this, their home. And, it is dedicated to the education of present and future generations with regard to a disease that has been shrouded in fear and ignorance for centuries."

—Hawaii Park Service brochure

A FRIEND OF a friend warned me. A woman who lived in a Honolulu ghetto and spoke thick pidgin cautioned before I boarded a plane for Molokai, that I'd find the real Hawaii there. Then she added, chortling, "It's just a rock, though. You can walk around it in a day."

When I saw that two passengers aboard the tiny island hopper carried ukuleles, I had a sense of what she was getting at, and the sound of her "ee" placed sweetly at the end of Molokai sang to me. But soon enough I'd learn that a Hawaii really does exist beyond the garishness of Waikiki's International Market Place. And it hovers ambiguously between deep Polynesia and, say, Lincoln, Nebraska—a lazy-eyed Midwestern emissary in the Pacific. It's slurping Budweiser with one hand and sucking poi from a plastic sack in the other. It's the macaroni salad drowning in mayonnaise with your ahi plate lunch. It's hanging on the tailgate of your beefed-up Ford, parked in front of your local reef point and throwing back some raw squid that your cousin caught. It's an old English-style tattoo reading "100% Moke". It's fried Spam and rice. It's plumeria plantations and grazing cattle. And its homeliness and violent beauty would give me all the heartbreak and excitement of coming upon a wrecked Iowan flatbed on a Polynesian highway.

FROM THE PLANE I saw the rock. It sat in the ocean like the crumbs of an ancient meal, but grew into a cragged mass as our plane shrank in its presence. From that distance, I guessed it would be an easy drive from one end to the other, but there was no way a human could walk around it in a day. Sea cliffs on the northern side—furrowed spires of black and green—propped up the flat mass of the island like a Cadillac on a jack stand. The northwest swell that I'd seen transformed to glory at Pipeline the day before was still running strong, oscillating in deep blues past Oahu and colliding with these north-facing cliffs. Ringed with white, and seemingly caught on the base of the cliffs like a buoyant water lily, the shrouded land of Kalaupapa was just visible. The plane banked. I could see the flat desert topside. Its tan was mottled by green squares of agriculture, abandoned cars rusting on their perimeters. The airport below was a slab of asphalt and a building—farms on either side.

Stepping off the plane (two steps), I noticed more travelers with cased ukuleles. They carried them like country Western singers of the '40s. Inside the airport was a small bar, a lei stand, a few idle people and an ironic banner that read "Molokai 2000". I wondered what would change here that hadn't in the last two millennia. That flight from Honolulu took about 20 minutes—a quick hop into another country.

Of course, the real Hawaii isn't a place people visit. It's a way people live. And for the most part, I never intended to go there. I'd come to Molokai with Matt Puder and George Puder—two brothers from Oahu. It was George's idea originally. His family had been donating building materials and time to Sisters of Mercy charities on Oahu. He made a few calls to the sisters and got us an invitation by Father Joseph to visit and stay at Kalaupapa—the historic leper colony on the northern central coast of Molokai.

Immediately, a kind of lust seeped into the idea. The attraction for us was the wave—theoretically, a heavy right positioned in the path of all that north swell. Its existence was hearsay to us at the time, but the access was certain to be difficult. There are only two ways to get down to Kalaupapa: one is a mule trail that scales Molokai's sea cliffs with 26 tedious switchbacks and the other is a daily six-seater that lands on a grass airstrip. Either way, someone of authority needs to meet you and escort you into the rest of the settlement. Later we learned leprosy patients were still living at Kalaupapa. The combination of the limited access, the dodgy circumstances and the feared disease gave the place an unnatural attraction.

ABOUT TWO CITY blocks long and lined with mom-and-pop stores, Kaunakakai's main drag bustled with weathered farm trucks and pampered Japanese four-wheel drives. High school kids in beaters monopolized the pay phone outside the market. There was a buzz like something was happening and you wondered where it could be on this small island. This was the metropolitan hub of the friendly island.

After sunset the Hotel Molokai is the only place a stranger can get a meal in Kaunakakai. It's an open-air dining patio with a bar. The chairs and tables sit on a cement slab maybe a foot or two above sea level. From any table, you can look across a calm channel at the island of Lanai. Large Hawaiian women wearing printed muumuus and flowers in their hair wade between the tables with a delicate grace. Ocean water laps just below the deck. I gazed past the tiki torches and over the water as the sun set—an idyllic place for the middle-aged vacationers who filled the other tables. It looked to me like something out of a brochure, and I had an inarticulate feeling of enduring it. Then, into my second beer, Matt leaned over and asked if I'd noticed anything unusual about the waitresses. I signaled our large waitress to order a third beer. It was nothing overt; she didn't have a mustache. But through the make-up and the hairdo, it became clear: she was a couple of hundred pounds of Hawaiian manhood. Mahu: a cultural anomaly. One local called them his "aunties"—these Hawaiian men raised to do the hula. Suddenly, the Hotel Molokai held a new charm and intrigue for me. The shock of a 300-pound man in a muumuu was reassuring.

It would be easy to float through a stay on Molokai and remember nothing but a sleepy island vacation. But the devil is in the details. When you begin to question the appearance of things, your tropical ease will run aground; your confidence will founder. For example, on every aisle of Misaki's grocery store were mounted deer heads. Furry and horned, they held starry-eyed dominion over the cereal boxes and canned goods. They hung in the liquor store—mounted above the soda pop and bagged poi on the counter. It seemed there was some kind of deer slaughtering going on and there weren't enough walls in town on which to mount their heads. Later in the evening I heard a guy parked in a four-wheel drive outside Misaki's saying he'd gotten six that day. I asked him about it, and he told me it was true. In an attempt at eradication, hunters were allowed to shoot as many deer as they could down at the leper colony. He said the deer had overrun the place, shitting everywhere and eating whatever they liked. Wild pig, too. But he said the pigs rooted in the patient's trash, and he wouldn't want to eat a pig from Kalaupapa and end up with knots all over his hands.

The hunter held up his hands as if to show where the sores would develop, and he laughed. More than 50 years had passed since the discovery of a cure for Hansen's disease, I thought, and there was still more than cliffs between the residents of Kalaupapa and the rest of the island. Only a couple of days later I'd hear the gun shots and glimpse the camouflaged hunters down at the settlement.

There are but 50 remaining leprosy patients in the community. The youngest is 60 and every year some pass on. For me, the ringing gunfire and the eradication of the deer signaled the ebbing of history. The sense that we were seeing the settlement a way it would never be again was pervasive. But Molokai proper was no more stable. Change was as determined as the trade winds.

"I WOULD SAY it's going off!" shouted a bodyboarder gimping along the highway. He was headed for the paddle-out spot, after taking a left far inside the point. His back was tattooed, his trunks sagged past his ass and he wore one fin—which made him waddle. But the smile, and the fact that he addressed us at all, we took as an invitation. This was a volcanic rock point, where the road swung wide to accommodate the coast. A gaggle of pickups and beater cars were parked hodge-podge along the road, and there were more locals hanging out there than in the water. Just off the point, a crystalline hip lumped up and spun left over a shallow reef.

We couldn't hide the fact that we were three honkies in a rental car. People lounging in their yards eyed our passing with what could only be described as disdain. As we passed the point before doubling back, guys sipping beers on their tailgates peered into our ride. It felt like slowly driving through Compton. But when George remembered the leftover twelve-pack in the car, we pulled over, sat on the bumper and cracked beers—a Jane Goodall approach to surfing. Then, like a couple of wusses, we asked the guys if we could surf their wave.

On the peak were mostly young bodyboarders. We paddled out and the session took on the mean-spirited joy of a free-for-all. The headland of Maui popped up just across the Pailolo Channel. Whales breeched between the two islands, and one jumped completely out of the water. Contrasting the dark vol-canic rocks that tumbled into the water at the point, the reef was a light green peppered with blues. The shallow water was but a bright veneer coating it. As the tide sucked out, and the wave became more bowly, I discovered the reef didn't feel nearly as beautiful as it looked. I caught road rash on my back, hands and feet. Getting caught inside, and with a ball of foam coming at him, George stood up on the reef, and the water he'd been pad-dling in came up to his shins. The wave was so consistent and ripable, though, that we kept tooling back out. The wind eased and the birthday waves started coming in.

Afterward we shot the shit with the boys on the highway, swapped stories and beers, and I tried some of the raw squid one of the boys caught. When we returned the next day, even the ladies and kiddies waved.

WE SAW A lot of graves. In fact, after Father Joseph picked us up from the grass airstrip at Kalaupapa, he drove along the road fronting the ocean. I could see hundreds of weathered graves divided by religion—Catholic, Buddhist, Protestant—all set in grass that carpeted this tongue of land at the base of Molokai's sea cliffs. Something like 7,000 people had died here over the past 150 hundred years, so we would see plenty more decaying handmade tombs. Many of them read simply, "Make"—Hawaiian for dead. Beyond these graves along the ocean were a few sparse trees, the beach, a hundred yards of shallow reef and, in the distance, a right point alive with swell. Father Joseph pointed out the graves as he drove, and I tried to glimpse, between tombstones and trees, the rights spooling down the reef. Father Joseph pulled abruptly onto the grass, stopped and pointed out a tree in the foreground. The tree's roots clutched a stone casket as though they had raised the casket right out of the ground. "The tree grew on top of the grave," Father Joseph said with a thick Belgian accent. "Come judgment day, the tree will have to be cut down before the man can come out." He laughed.

In a stand of markers dividing the Buddhist tombs was a vacant grave that had been full the week before. The grave had belonged to a Chinese man dead some 91 years. One of his distant relatives had a dream and in it was told the patriarch no longer wished to exist at the settlement. The week before I arrived, the family came and collected his remains and took them home to Honolulu. Father Joseph shrugged and shook his head as he told the story.

I lamented not having a camera. Father Joseph poked his forehead with a bony white finger. "In your mind, in your memory, you will keep these things." A handful of the small Indian deer ran across the road, and we passed a homemade sign that read: "Smile. It no broke your face."

As we drove, almost vertical, deeply furrowed cliffs towered over us. It is said that the land here came from a separate volcanic event than those that created the majority of the island, including Molokai's northern palisades. The land above the cliffs is called "topside" by locals—a world away.

At the height of the leper population, the sheerness of the cliffs inspired another name for Kalaupapa: the living tomb. In the earliest days the place was so grim that ships transporting new arrivals anchored just off shore and literally pushed them into the water. Now, the tomb looks like a combination of Gettysburg and a country-style island paradise—graves, greenery, ocean. The patients' few cars and trucks are left with keys in the ignitions; there are no locks on the doors of the homes. At the impromptu neighborhood bar, residents pay for their drinks when they have the money. There is a meeting hall where residents exact a meticulous control over their settlement.

There came a time, after leprosy began to be curable in the

mid-'40s, when the residents of Kalaupapa were given a choice many never expected to have: to stay or go. Suddenly, the physical barriers that held them eroded away, and mental and social barriers exposed themselves. Some patients were weary of how the outer world would receive them—deformities and all. But more powerful, this place had become their home. For most, there was nowhere to go.

"LOOK AT THAT one." We sat at a picnic table on the beach. At our left, Molokai's palisades extended skyward and into the distance—corrugated folds of lava. The beach extended to our right. For yards out from the beach were the crags and the rock heads of a shallow bottom, then the rocks dropped away and, just outside, the waves broke. The farthest point took the brunt of the swell, forming lumped up bombs. Three more distinct rights lay between our picnic table and the point. The waves at each peak diminished in size—the farthest inside was a fun wedging right; the farthest outside was an uncertain cloudbreak. The two between spit and chewed along the shallow bottom. There were no people anywhere.

There was a pall over this beauty. We just found out after months of planning that the local sheriff, a patient himself, decided we couldn't surf, or dive, or pick opihi. It seemed arbitrary. Each of us felt a pinch of bitterness. This feeling of being cheated mixed with stranger emotions. The wave cracking offshore from this cemetery drove home a sharp idea: an event of profound humanity happened in this place. Coming here singularly to surf, well, I felt as though we'd gone to Hiroshima to surf, or Auschwitz. We could have easily charged out there, but this barrier, of respect or foreboding, was as distinct a condition as weather or geography.

A white Ford pickup had pulled onto the grass where it met the sand. A small, slightly stooped Japanese Hawaiian man stepped out and slammed the door. He wore a baseball cap, T-shirt, jeans and fishing boots. His face lacked expression. I thought we'd done something forbidden—kapu—and he'd come to chastise us about it. But then he sat down as though we were longtime pals and said, "I've lived in Hawaii for 70 years, and I never learned to surf." The four of us looked out as the next set came filing in, stacking and spitting.

As though remembering something, I turned to the old man, examining his face. First, I thought it was age, his lack of expression. Soon I learned it was leprosy that paralyzed the muscles in his face, filling in his features like a full tide. The skin of his face and arms was spotted, but like that of someone who had spent a lifetime in the sun.

"You guys are surfers," he said. There was no need to respond: I'd gotten used to the idea that our presence preceded us the way it would in any small town.

When I think of the way it started, I wish I'd recorded this conversation because it was one of the most amazing things I'd ever heard. I don't know exactly when the talk turned from water, reefs and swell into the story of his life, but it happened as easily and as naturally as anything.

His name was Paul, he said, and he'd been living at Kalaupapa since he was 16. Now 70, he mentioned there were many patients here who didn't like to talk about their illness, or what it had been like to have been sent here. One woman, in particular, continued to grieve having been snatched away from a fiancé, would talk only grudgingly and became irate at the sight of a camera.

Paul grew up on Kauai and had 10 brothers and sisters—all living. He talked about catching fish in a river by his parents' farm, and what it had been like when his friends began to call him "Jap" in the days just before Pearl Harbor. He doesn't know how he contracted Hansen's disease (because they don't like being called lepers), but it appeared as a white spot on his forearm where the skin no longer perspired. At the time he thought the white spot had something to do with work in the rice paddies. In his early teens, he was sent to way stations before landing at Kalaupapa. These two events, his childhood friends turning on him and the stigma of the disease, mingled in his thoughts. Then, he said what a terrible burden racism and fear were, and despite his troubles, at least he didn't have to carry that burden. "I'm an underdog, being an underdog is wonderful."

He looked around the beach, and for him, it was full of memory. He pointed out where he liked to net fish. Where he'd once seen a shark near his boat. "And over there, while diving, I saw a sea bass that was this big," he said stretching out his arms. "And, with all the little fish around him, well, it looked like the moon dragging along the stars. It was a sight to behold."

"Do you know what leprosy is?" he asked during a lull in conversation, showing us his hands. The hands were worn like a fisherman's and strong, despite the missing thumbs. He explained the disease in terms of his life and mobility. He hadn't had problems with his feet like some patients did. His thumbs were amputated, though, and he described how it happened. Paul was married, but he and his wife decided not to have children because at the time, the state's policy was to remove newborns from the custody of inflicted parents. "The beautiful thing about it, though, is that children are born without leprosy, they don't have it."

Soon enough, the four of us were loaded into his truck and driving closer to the point on an erstwhile surf check. I sat in the truck's bed with Paul's fishing gear.

At the point, just inside the break, a rusted post thrust maybe 15 feet out of the water. On Christmas Eve, 1932, Paul said, the crossing from Honolulu to Molokai had been a grueling feat for this freighter. So much so, that when it entered the calmer waters near Kalaupapa, the crew began to celebrate Christmas and their lives. They drank so hard, none remembered to drop the anchor. The boat drifted into the lineup and was crushed at the point by the waves we came to surf. Now, only the post revealed the ship underneath. It looked like a good point of reference to lineup with.

When Paul dropped us off at Father Joseph's, he said we'd really made a mistake by visiting the father and not him. "If you'd come to visit me, you'd be surfing out there right now."

BY COINCIDENCE, A dozen of our new friends from the left point on the east side were in the airport bar to see a friend off. The friend decided he didn't want to leave Molokai after all, so it became our impromptu farewell party. We drank, talked and shared Pulani's dried fish until it was necessary to board the twin engine to Honolulu. The flight was full, so I got to sit next to the pilot. When the engines were buzzing, and we taxied down the runway, the pilot pointed and said, "Is that for you?" Our east side friends had driven up to a bluff at the end of the runway and were waving from the beds and roofs of their trucks. I watched them until the plane banked west over the ocean. Swell was again pulsing from the north. I thought about the wave at Kalaupapa, but it wasn't the bittersweet emotion of the one that got away. The wave will always be there, but Kalaupapa will never be this way again—nor will the real Hawaii.

The Apaches:

Los Mexicanos on the North Shore

RIDING DOWN HIGHWAY 83, sitting shotgun in David Rutherford's $600 Toyota Celica, a fleeting illusion took me: this was May of 2000, and I was in Mexico again. Through the windshield, an afternoon light padded the roadside greenery so beautifully it made me bleary-eyed. Omar Diaz and Celestino Diaz rapped softly in Spanish as we passed a large shade tree with three horses under its canopy. Country smells blew through the windows.

This temporal displacement only lasted an instant though. As the Toyota we rode in approached the Haleiwa turnoff on the North Shore of Oahu, the thought of Mexico evaporated like something we'd driven through.

"Fifty pesos a day," Celestino said finally in English. "That's a lot of money."

He was talking about the cost of three round meals from the aisles of Foodland, a grocery chain located only in the islands. Two thousand miles away in his hometown of Puerto Escondido, Mexico, it is an obscene amount to spend on food. But the very idea that he and his friends David and Omar were here on the North Shore of Oahu, amazingly plopped in the middle of the Pacific, Celestino said, "Is like a dream."

In reality, this was December 10, 2000, and just that morning trials for the Pipeline Masters had begun. Because of the crowds it attracted, the four of us were heading to the other side of Haleiwa for a surf. Seventeen-year-old David was driving the first car he'd ever owned—the Toyota he bought with cash on arrival in Hawaii three weeks before.

By the teeth-grinding sound the Toyota made as we slowed for a bus, it was obvious the car's brake pads were dangerously worn. David was only slightly concerned, but noted that the car didn't seem to stop as well as it had when he first bought it. I asked if he had some kind of international driver's license. David chuckled.

"Just like Mexico," Omar piped in from the back. "No license, but plenty of experience."

This was the first time these talented surfers had been to the North Shore—an essential leap for any ambitious young surfer. The incredible part is the length of time it took a true Puerto Escondido contingent, surfers known for their ease in hollow waves, to arrive here. Brazilians, Puerto Ricans, Europeans, just about any nation with waves has seen its surfers perform and mature on the North Shore. Before these guys, only one Puerto Escondido mentor, Coco Nogales, made the trip—returning to relay the island surf's nuances.

Yet, resources for a serious Mexican campaign were—and are—lacking. There is no internal support for young surfers, like the National Scholastic Surfing Association in the United States, for example, and the country's best surfers miss out on the kind of financial support that fuels the ambitions of other foreign pros.

"We don't have the same help in Puerto," David said. "You don't start as a surfer from your parents. You just pick it up at the beach. Surfers here have a lot of help."

"We're here, but it took a long ways," Celestino said, waving his hand in agreement.

Oddly, despite the poverty of their country, at 21 years old both Omar and Celestino were well-traveled—even if in the past it required paying a coyote to get that way. When Celestino was just 15, he crossed the U.S. border illegally using the age-old custom of paying a "guide." From the border he traveled as far north as Santa Cruz where he glassed and sanded boards for Arrow. He surfed all along the coast, but was finally caught unaware while checking the surf in Redondo Beach—by a cop who thought the teenager was playing hooky.

A year later Celestino won the Mexican national junior division and his good friend Omar was runner-up. This got them an invitation to a 1996 International Surfing Association competition in Huntington, along with letters to the U.S. embassy in Mexico City. With the letters, the young athletes were able to get "one-entry" visas. This meant they were allowed to enter the United States for the express purpose of competing. The two grommets did enter the United States, but that is when things got a little shady. Instead of competing, they took jobs at a palm tree farm for $300 a week.

They worked that job a month and a half. The purchase made with the princely sum was two round-trip tickets to Indonesia. They surfed Nias, Bawa, G-land and Bali. For each of them, at 16 years old, it was a trip that would have made Gulliver proud. The kicker is, once they arrived back in Los Angeles, they were immediately deported to Mexico for improperly using their visas. "That was cool, man," Omar said somewhat resigned. "We wanted to go home anyway."

This trip to the North Shore was different though—more of a pilgrimage than an escape. For one, David, Omar and Celestino now carried the necessary papers for extensive travel. "That was one of our goals," Omar said. "Now we have papers, and we can travel to other countries." Secondly, their American sponsors picked up part of the travel expenses—somewhat of a milestone for Puerto Escondido surfers.

For each of them the experience has been like walking into the pages of the surf magazines. "It's like a meeting," said Omar, describing the North Shore during the Triple Crown. "It's an opportunity to see all those guys. And we want to show them that the Mexicans can surf."

"Ha! That the Apaches can surf!" Celestino said.

Many of the pros out in the celebrity lineups already knew this. Even though the Mexican's faces are new to Pipe, for many of the pros out there, they aren't strange. The Mexicans meet every traveling surfer who arrives in Mexico during Puerto's summertime swells. And for anyone who has surfed there, these guys are easily recognized. During a session out at Pipe, Davey Miller noticed that Celestino's wave count was nearly nonexistent. Miller used his hierarchy in the lineup to paddle for waves, but then gave them to Celestino. The flip side to being that well-recognized is that those who have experienced Puerto's brand of localism remember the surfers also. One Pipe local asked Celestino if he felt "comfortable in the lineup."

Celestino answered, "Yes, I'm having a good time."

"I didn't feel comfortable in Puerto," the local said. "And I don't want you to feel too comfortable here."

David, Omar and Celestino agreed: they thought cracking the hierarchy and getting some Puerto-size barrels would be easier. "No way," they said. "It's like, 'Hit the showers.'"

When we reached the break just off of a small country neighborhood that day, the guys kept marveling at the beauty of the place. The waves were smallish, but the water was a very clear blue. Wind only slightly peppered its surface. It looked like the kind of water out of which turtles might rise at any time. Behind us, sloping farmland gave way to steep green mountainside. "It's so beautiful," Celestino said. "Look up there." From the water, Celestino pointed to the lava mountain's pinnacle. "That one huge tree all alone on the top of the mountain—it's so big," he said, amazed. On the distant, uppermost part of the mountain, we could see the thing standing resolute. Not wanting to change the place for

Celestino, I didn't have the heart to tell him that the old grand-father of a tree was really a military satellite dish.

But later on, driving back down the country road in the $600 Toyota, I think the guys came to their own conclusions about this place and their own. Looking out the window Celestino said, "Hawaii is good, but Puerto is good, too."

"Yes, Puerto is good, too," David and Omar agreed.

In the Dirt

"TELL THE GROM to hold on," Sonny Miller yells from the back of the boat. My heart sinks into my shoes and I grasp the rail with white knuckles. The little boat crests yet another open-ocean swell and begins to drop. I look forward to see the "grom," Mike Morrissey, floating in the air a foot above his seat. He's facing the sea. His red windbreaker has expanded in the wind like a balloon. He's desperately trying to hold on to loose boards at either side of him, but they're floating haphazardly above the bow, too, threatening to fly away. Then, half of the boat slams into the trough of the swell with a sickening, hull-shattering sound. This is followed by the sound of Mike crumpling like a wooden marionette onto the bench he'd been sitting on and the chattering of boards as they're racked against the bow. I briefly wonder if the hull of the boat has survived just as we begin to sputter up the face of another wave.

Behind me, the boat's owner mutters in Spanish, "This is worse than I thought." Wind is blowing hard against our faces. There is water pouring off the brim of my hat and dripping over my sunglasses. I can barely see, but I turn to look for the land we left behind, wondering if I could swim back the way we came. On most surf trip boat rides, I've taken solace in the idea that, yes, if I had to, I could swim back. But the little fishing village is just a speck now. The island we're headed for is just a rock in the distance. In between is a deep-water channel with currents streaming to God knows where. I think, unnervingly, no, it's too far to swim back, and it's too far to make the island.

My heart has begun to rise back into place when I hear Donavon Frankenreiter yelling. He's wearing a hooded sweatshirt with the its drawstring pulled into a small circle revealing only his sunglasses. The entire sweatshirt is soaked, and water is running over his lenses. As we reach the next peak, Bret Strother is also yelling, no words, just, "Ahhh!" The bow of the boat falls away, my heart sinks into my shoes—again—and the grom is left hanging mid-air. When the bow slams into the trough, water washes over us—over our meager clothing, down our legs and into our shoes with our hearts. But the water, by now, hardly matters. The boat owner turns to Sonny and says he can't believe no one has puked. Bret screams, "Ahhh, we went from a shitty dirt road to an even shittier boat ride."

It's been said that on the road, there is no such thing as adventure and romance, only trouble and desire. There is no sense of mystery, only of confusion. Nowhere is this truer than the capillaries off Mexico's Highway 1 in the bowels of Baja California. The earliest maps of Baja illustrated it as a rugged island unto itself. And despite the fact that a road crew working south from Tijuana met a road crew working north, completing the highway at Santa Ynez in

1973, Baja is still a rugged island.

Crossing the border at Tijuana and heading south past the beaches before Ensenada, however, isn't the cultural shock it once was. Hoards of American retirees' homes and tourist developments have given the northernmost part of Baja the look of a budding San Clemente. Cornfields and shanties along the road have given way to condos and gated estates. The new homes are painted in pastels and off-whites and are topped with enormous satellite dishes. There are uniquely American problems here now, too. The week before we drove this road, a sniper set up a perch overlooking the highway near Baja Malibu. The gunman began to shoot long-range at what were described as "late model" cars with California license plates. Mexican police tracked down an armed suspect a day later. The man they detained was from Orange County, and it was suggested that he didn't like "rich Americans."

This small-scale American colonialism and Jimmy Buffet existence ends abruptly at Ensenada. The port is busy here, and the smell is powerful. Colorful fish-taco stands lining the alleys of the port are a relief from the road. There is nothing here to imply it, but this cluster of buildings and boats is the place where surfers headed to Todos Santos negotiate a ride. As our two-car caravan navigated this side street, I thought of cold-water mornings and surfers unloading their big-wave guns in the soft predawn light, slipping out to sea. Ours was a summertime trip, though, and we were traveling much deeper down.

At the south end of Ensenada, a military checkpoint signals an entirely different Baja. Soldiers who would still be unable to get a driver's permit in the United States wave us past with the butts of assault rifles. We followed a train of semis up a rise and out of town. On the other side is a river valley furrowed by vineyards. This is the last significant patch of green before the Vizcaino Desert.

The agricultural expanse was new to our photographer, Aaron Loyd, who first made this drive in 1979. Aaron is a veteran of this road. He still limps from an injury sustained in a car accident here during one of his initial trips. But he said the roads are better now, without as many potholes, and a bit wider. "It used to be a 14-foot-wide ribbon running through the country. It's safer now and has a shoulder here and there. But you still have to watch out for cows," he warned.

Gradually the desert evolves from a chaparral into a cactus garden more crowded and diverse than the one outside your grandma's Palm Springs trailer. Following turns defined by a cliff at either side, you'll notice there are no guardrails. The road's treachery is confirmed when you see the charred cars at random intervals and the santo shrines that dot the shoulder—there to mourn the many roadside tragedies. Clusters of rounded boulders and stands of barrel cactus are often graffittied with names: Lupe, Miguel, Carlos. Oddly, the bad graffiti doesn't bother you the way it would somewhere else. It's a welcome relief of color in an otherwise blighted landscape.

Semi trucks lean over the yellow line, seeming to say, "It's me or you." And when push comes to shove, you know it's you. So, of course you move over, and a wave of heat and wind push your car around like a toy.

Coming upon slower traffic, the car ahead will sometimes flash its left blinker. This means it's clear, as far as that driver can see, to pass. It's a matter of trust. Near dusk, blazing through the cactus and boulder garden, we came up fast on an old Toyota. The car was pretty beat up, but its left blinker worked, and we made our move to pass. Pulling parallel to the Toyota, I could see the car was windowless and stuffed with people and boxes. The driver, unbelievably, was wearing a "halo," a device worn by people with severe neck injuries. It was surreal. This is the kind of place that will force a man with a broken neck to load up his car and keep on moving. The sun set, and a sliver of the moon hung at the edge of the darkest blue, chasing after the sun. Venus, brighter than a star, hung like a beauty mark just above the horizon. The growing night gave the desert an aquatic atmosphere—bluffs and mesas became reefs; cactus became sea life.

"Brake, brake, brake," Donavon's voice cracked over the radio. He rode in the car ahead, but was out of view. "Brake!" Rounding a curve we saw the Suburban's brake lights flaring, and then it swerved into the oncoming lane and back again. What then filled the expanse of our headlights was a Brahman bull two-thirds the size of our SUV. It didn't move from the center of the road.

We braked.

"Moo," Donavon called out over the radio. "Moo."

WAKING UP AT Abreojos is like waking up at Lowers and pad-
dling out with a few of your friends. Except here, you'd take your
time, maybe have a cup of coffee, pick the dirt out of your teeth
and do your "paperwork." And once out in the lineup, you're not
looking over your shoulder to see an army of hungry surfers suiting
up on the beach. But the place is by no means desolate. When we
arrived, there were a few sets of campers along the main point: fishermen, windsurfers, outlaws on the lam. There was also a half-
dozen or so vacant shacks and trailers left here by surfers. A dirt
runway on the other side of a rise accommodated about a plane a
day, sometimes piloted by surfers.

The oddest thing about being in the morning lineup is the sun
rising out of the ocean. Abreojos belongs to a handful of "banana
points" along the coast of North America. The land loops around
until its tip is facing east. This is also the reason light offshore
winds begin about noon and quickly pick up into a maddening
crescendo, settling an hour after the sun has set. There are four or
five rights lining about a mile of land here. We renamed the first
point "Burgers," but it was consistently a couple of feet bigger than
the rest. Razors, the flower of the bunch, roped in at a constant
barreling speed. Light offshores feathered all 2 feet of its face
before the wave crashed onto dry rock. The wave looked perfect

and, at the time, too small to be ridable. Bret and Mike leered at the wave, willing it to grow. "Look at this one. Look at this set." The wave would rope in as small as the others and crash onto dry rock. "That one was ridable."

Our first surf after the drive was a pleasure. The water was cool and seemed to wash the miles of traveling away. It wasn't big, but occasional sets were head high, and it hinted at picking up. We all thought we were in for something good. The sun rose high above the water, and the offshores made the waves a little more racy. Then, suddenly, the wind picked up speed like a locomotive and blew the waves back out to sea. We set up camp in that wind, laboring to erect our tents. Twenty minutes after Bret and Mike got theirs set up, the wind snapped its fiberglass supports, and the tent fell over like a wounded bird.

Our afternoons were spent in refuge from the sun and wind. A lazy drive in Sonny's Suburban through Abreojos proper, a Tecate between the legs, waving to people from the windows and receiving more *holas* than a prom queen. Maybe we'd stop by and pick up a block of ice or some freshly made tortillas. A truck passed by with an 8-foot shark in the back. We spotted a local beauty walking alone down the road. We watched the heat shimmer in the distance. It was slow living.

One afternoon we attended a local ball game: Abreojos versus La Bocana. There was mariachi music between innings and five-peso beers. Cars and trucks surrounded the outfield. People sat on hoods shouting to a cousin or a brother in the game. The players whipped the ball around the bases after every play.

The only thing stronger than the wind was the flies. These animals, I shit you not, were the diameter of a dime. They had more command of the wind than the pair of sea hawks that perched on the tower above Razors. They could fly straight into the wind and do loops. A fly once jumped into Bret's rum and coke. It didn't move. Bret thought it was dead, so he pick the fly out and tossed it. Mid-toss, the thing flew off, a happy *borracho*. There was a bush near camp that I thought had berries on it. The berries turned out to be flies. At one point, I hadn't taken a dump in a couple of days, and I had no idea where everyone was taking care of business. I asked Donavon what the procedure was. He said, "Take that shovel, go way out there and dig a deep hole. Afterward, make sure to bury your shit, or the flies will get to it and then come back here and give us hepatitis. Bury your shit deep." I began to fear the flies.

The morning sessions at the main point were the best. We could surf or not, maybe eat breakfast instead and then surf. Sometimes, we'd get three sessions in before the wind picked up. The sunny, windy afternoons were simply endured. One afternoon Mike, Bret and Donavon decided it was time to give 2-foot Razors a try. They sat in the lineup 5 feet from the rocks. They paddled for occasional set waves. Some of the waves wouldn't let them in; they would warble a bit and crash onto the rocks. Now and again, one of the guys would drop into a winner and get a tiny, perfect tube just a foot or two off of the rocks. During the 20-minute session, each one of them broke a fin out of their boards. That afternoon a couple of us sat in 3 feet of shade created by one of the vehicles. The wind was torrential enough to carry off a small child. Reflectively, slowly, our weathered photographer, Aaron, said of the rest of us, "These guys don't have a clue about Baja. I've been here for weeks when it was windier than this. I'd just go find a rock somewhere and sit behind it."

THEN CAME THE decision. We'd gleaned everything we could from this rock point, and a new swell was coming—we were convinced. There is a certain kind of desperation that drives a person to pack up and move on with no good reason. We were infected by it, swell or not. Where to go? Scorpion Bay? Cabo?

The decision brought us 200 miles north on a desert road. In transit, four boards flew off the roof of one car. Two of the boards were returned by a pair of laughing farmers in a truck 20 miles down the road. Two of the boards were gone for good. Then, one of the cars ran out of gas and got a flat. We bounced into Punta Eugenia—dusty and road-worn—and it felt as though we'd stumbled into Popeye's fishing village. There were clusters of small homes, a small lighthouse and a small bay with several boats in it. Our journey wasn't finished. The six of us piled into a fishing boat for a short $20 boat ride.

Steinbeck passed by these islands in a 76-foot purse seiner

during the early '40s. It's the last description in his book *The Log from the Sea of Cortez.* "The *Western Flyer* hunched into the great waves toward Cedros Island: the wind blew off the tops of the whitecaps, and the big guy wire, from bow to mast, took up its vibration like the low pipe on a tremendous organ. It sounded its deep note into the wind."

The crossing lasted an hour, and Mike spent much of it airborne. Although we'd been yelling and not singing, the boat ride seemed to complete us. By then we were more wind, water and dirt than anything else. Through adversity, we'd stopped fighting our tendency for trouble, desire and confusion. Accepting it became the adventure, the fun. We'd gone from a shitty road to a shittier boat ride, and as we entered the calm waters around Isla Natividad, we were laughing. It helped us to see the beauty of this place.

The wind and waves lessened as we crossed to the inside of the kelp bed. We passed a huge rock, set like a sentry just off the island. The water nearest the island's dark cliffs was glassy, sparkling and a cobalt blue. Birds flew low in formation over the water and the cliffs. The island was called Afegua, or island of birds, by the Cochimi tribe who first inhabited it. And the birds seemed to be its masters.

A collection of homes and buildings sits on the island's southeast corner. Sonny had been here 16 years before. There may be a few more houses now, he said, but it hadn't changed much. We unloaded our gear from the boat, hiked up to town and found a truck to take us across the island.

It was obvious the homes belonged to fishermen and to urchin and abalone divers. From the truck, we saw their beaver-tail wetsuits hanging on clotheslines. There was a lighthouse set on tan, rolling hills that fell away at the cliff shore. We drove down a dirt airstrip that ran out to the beach. The afternoon brought on an orange glow the guys were calling the "golden hour." For such a famous beach, it's smaller than you'd expect, bordered by rock and only about 100 yards long. But immediately, I noticed how utterly exposed it is to open ocean. As soon as the truck reached the sand, a set of four or five A-frame peaks rifled across the spit of sand.

When I got out of the truck, something pulled hard at my back—another cursedly strong offshore wind. Once again, there would be no way to erect the tents until long after dark. We'd have to use rocks to hold our gear down. The sun was beginning to set, and still, the wind hurled over the rolling hills at our backs, feathered the tops of the fun-sized waves and continued blowing out across the dark blue channel. At any minute, an army of flies was going to cross the channel like a fleet of B-52s. I was sure of it.

Banchong and the Bemo

MIDWAY THROUGH OUR paranoid escape from Muslim Java, our crowded minibus bumped a motorbike right off the road and just kept rollicking on forward. The motorbike rider had been attempting to punch through the inside lane—a risky, yet popular tactic on these deadly Indonesian roads. Tragically, in what was merely a hallway cut through the jungle, the road narrowed just as our *bemo* swayed like a lumbering elephant. Both the motorbike and its rider bounced off our broadside like playthings, trundling fantastically off the shoulder. The effect seemed related more to the physics of air hockey than auto wrecks.

Our Balinese driver had gone pale for fractions of a second as he watched the rearview mirror become a theater of limbs and bike parts flying and spinning. Then, instinctively, he applied more of his foot to the gas pedal. As he did this, flush returned to his face as rapidly as the gas injected into the engine. Wayan knew, as we all did, that to pull over would be to subject himself and passengers to the will of the Javanese family certain to pop out of the forest. In a country unfamiliar with the rule of law, apparent justice is meted out swiftly to those moral enough to pull over and accept it.

I'd taken this same route three times before—from G-land to Kuta Beach, between Islamic Java and Hindu Bali. Luckily, two of the trips occurred at night when I was unable to witness the slaughter that is Indonesian road travel. The experience, via *bemo* and ferry, is physically nauseating. But because of political forces outside our control, this specific journey, this escape, became more emotional than physical.

Wayan and I had become pals in Pantai Kuta. Really, I'd only stumbled upon him and his partner sipping large Bintangs on the sidewalk and joined them. We joked about the jiggy-jig and laughed at sun burnt German tourists. That acquaintance gave me the unfortunate distinction of sitting shotgun. I didn't want to sit on the bench seat next to Wayan, nor did I feel like a wuss because of it, knowing that our chances of survival as a whole had little to do with where I sat. Although, the same could not be said for the large South African in back, the displacement of his girth could have had potential consequences as to the trajectory of our vehicle. The shotgun position here in Indonesia is like a seat placed not on the periphery of the bullring, but inside it. I'd still be sitting, but I would no longer be a spectator. Just beyond the windshield would pass life's most barren third-world realities. I knew that any of it had the ability to wreak havoc within the cab. So, as we began on that early September morning, my fears and swallowed complaints churned and rattled in my chest like the rocks trapped in the *bemo*'s hubcaps.

Here is the thing: through the big windshield that particular morning, the countryside looked something close to paradise. The heads of distant, foreboding volcanoes dipped in and out of lofty clouds. And below, in their deep blue shadow, stately palms arranged themselves into rows, dividing the terraced greens of one rice paddy from another. While I was flying above sometime later, the rice paddies below sparkled and reflected the sunshine like shards of a neatly broken mirror. Near the road, plumeria trees stood guard outside modest homes of ornate brick and tile. There were idle bulls in fields guarded by officious scarecrows. There were small Islamic mosques and wandering roosters and children in school uniforms. A few minutes into the ride, a large rice paddy opened intermittently to the road. A small woman stood up out of an emerald green terrace that wavered like a rippling lake—a rattan hat shading the face that watched us pass.

What forever separated this place from paradise were the forces at work on the gut. Let your senses imagine an odor: something like one part wafting clove cigarette, eight parts potent diesel exhaust and a minutia of plumeria fragrance—an utterly sweet toxicity. It's a complex smell. A newcomer might be fooled into thinking the occasional dead dog at the side of the road had a part in it. A nose unfamiliar with its ingredients may have discerned only the voluminous spent fuel—visible remnants of which created a dirty haze obscuring distant vistas of beauty. The smell alone was enough to make a man puke.

But this odor was buffeted and harried along by the sound of the place—the thunder of missing tailpipes and rattling manifolds.

Automobile horns were used not in discretion or out of rage, but as a means of communicating every move—the constant irreverent honking an entire language unto itself, a language composed of one word blurted out artlessly into infinity. The mooning of cows and clucking of cocks drowned in it like bits of egg in fried noodle soup. The blaze of the South Sea wind passed as inaudible as it was invisible. The sound was brilliant.

Yet, most irredeemable among obstacles between this place and the illusion of paradise lay the road itself. Motorists negotiated its ramshackle lay with the deftness of rats eager to usurp another's position. Just as often as not, and at speed, decisions were made entirely at the expense of other motorists. It was the rule of the jungle as interpreted by modern transportation. The big trucks ruled, and when they came on fast, the lesser vehicles scattered. When they slowed, others dodged around them with the agility of the lower food chain. Road signs were as allusive as road workers, mounds of asphalt obstructing the road as likely as car-sized pits subtracted from it, dead dogs as numerous as vehicle wreckage. The Indonesian word for "sick," being the same for "broken," suggests that all things may become well on their own, a method of thinking that leaves no need for the word "maintenance."

My new friend Wayan wore a puff of black hair on his head like a mink fur hat. This hair helmet seemed secured to his crown by a matching goatee strapped to his chin. Between chin and hair was a mischievous, easily smiling face with dark sparkling eyes and teeth that, had I known better, were suspect to ornamental sharpening. His arms, sleeved to the shoulders with vibrant Balinese tattoos, pulled at the steering wheel as though prudence was a custom as foreign to his Hindu land as Christmas.

As an inter-island driver, Wayan earned something close to 80 bucks a month. Twice a week, he drove for nearly 20 hours a stretch, catching a nod only during the short ferry crossing between Bali and Java and back again. It was a good job, he said. He was 27, and he'd been driving this route for four years. In the hotels of Bali, he could earn maybe $20 a month and as a mechanic working seven days a week, maybe $75. There was also the prestige of being an inter-island traveler, of knowing and working for cool Western surfers and of having pocket money. Plus there was the thrill of the job. And I suspect a certain satisfaction gleaned from the faces of passengers who thought him a complete "nutter," as the Aussies accused him several times. While passing a brigade of motorbikes loaded to the hilt with chickens crammed into rattan baskets, a feather-blown aviary on wheels, Wayan faked left and careened right as easily as he faked through our conversations in English—smiling and nodding and going about his job with speed and recklessness.

The extremely large and awkward South African seated in the far back blurted, at monotonous intervals, "Driver, I want a nice beer and some nice snacks. Pull over." The phrasing of his words suggested that he'd spared Wayan and the rest of us the "Bloody

Kaffir" that would have fit neatly into the sentence had he been back home in Cape Town. Wayan drove on. None of the other passengers, two Argentines and two Australians, spoke. I could see the grin on Wayan's face and the gleam in his eye that looked something like a defiant country boy's. I laughed inside at his fleeting English comprehension whenever this South African spoke. I wanted a nice beer as well. A large Bintang could ease the sway and bump in the road. Two bottles could transpose one to an easy Sunday drive with sunshine and a light breeze. But what I wanted more just then was to feel the large South African suffer in want of that beer. "Hey, you, small American," he barked at me, "tell the boy I want a beer."

I looked back between the seats as though his English was hackneyed. He glared, his dark eyes as insolent as two olives pressed into a gob of freckled dough. I turned back and thought of mentioning the South African's desires; Wayan's lips split into a malicious smile. "This is khack," the South African said finally. Indeed, we passed through several small towns dotted with markets advertising cold amber Bintang.

Maybe it wasn't just me, though; maybe all of us felt the ineptitude of celebration during that time. This trip, in essence, was not the happy return it should have been. It was an escape. And for me it was worlds away from the first. I was running away from a beautiful Islamic country to a nation at war, and it didn't feel right really. And I'm not sure it felt necessary either. I gleaned the details of

the road and the world—texture, smell, color, cackle and clang—
with the somber clarity that I once experienced as a teenager on
the way home from a funeral. The first trip here I felt like a traveler
moving through the world. This time I sat stationary, the world
moved passed and I studied it.

THE REASONS FOR this began two weeks before when I sat at a
not-so-sturdy plastic table overlooking the pale blue waters of
Sanur Harbor. I felt for the moment in control of where I was
going. I had a ticket in my hand, and I could see the idle ferry to
Lembongan beached and waiting. Traditionally dressed men carrying fighting cocks in baskets walked past and loaded the birds onto
the small public ferry. Some European tourists lingered in the open
air café, and several locals and travelers sat on the beach waiting for
the same boat. I ordered coffee, a jaffle and a mixed juice from a
pretty waitress wearing a detailed sarong and a lace top. An Israeli
man, who looked something like a darker Woody Allen, sat at the
only other table on this patch of dirt just before the sea. My jaffle
and coffee arrived, and as I began to eat, one of the men who'd
been carrying the fighting cocks yelled to me, "The boat is going
to leave."

"It's just now 10 o'clock," I said. "The boat isn't to leave
until 10:30."

He said the boat leaves now. I signaled the waitress and asked
for a bill, asking her to bring my coffee in a cup to go. The

remorseful-looking Israeli at the other table said something imprecise as I began to rise. Absentmindedly, I asked, "What's that?"

He said, "The planes. Do you know about the planes which crashed into the World Trade Center?"

"What are you talking about?"

"Yes, two hijacked planes flew into the World Trade Center in New York. The buildings collapsed," he said. "Ten thousand people are dead."

I couldn't quite process what he'd said to me at that moment. "Palestinians," he added with emphasis. "There will be a war."

The other ferry passengers had already boarded. Both the passengers and the man with the fighting cocks began yelling at me to hurry. The pretty waitress appeared from behind me and slipped a warm plastic bag into my hand. It was my coffee poured into a sandwich bag and tied in a knot at the top. The Israeli looked at me, maybe at my despondence, and asked, "Are you American?"

"Yes," I said.

"You'd better call your family."

The ferry passengers hollered more vehemently, and I hobbled down to the beach with my backpack, surfboard and coffee in a bag. I waded through the dirty water between the beach and the ferry, asking the first passenger I came to, "What do you know about hijacked planes and the World Trade Center?" He looked at me with blank eyes.

"I don't speak English," he said brokenly.

As it happened, one of the biggest swells of the dry season was running that day, forcing our tiny boat to skirt land. Hill-sized lumps of the cleanest blue rolled the boat rather gently, considering the distances we rose and fell. We could see the power of this swell manifested in explosions of white once the oscillating lumps ran aground on distant islands. The green of the islands rising above the explosions seemed a product of them. The sky above was so lofty, the clouds so courageous, the immediacy and the reality of our little boat's precarious situation only lent the day a still dreamier quality.

An Italian couple, a scruffy man and an attractive younger woman sat on the bench behind mine. The woman was terrified of the boat and of the immensity of water in the Badung Strait. She was probably the only sensible one among us. She spoke no English, but the man knew a little. We began talking, but mostly we used crude hand gestures. Too soon, the conversation became this new tragedy we were barely aware of. Our arms became the Twin Towers, our hands became jet planes and, after the very barest of facts, we could no longer communicate. My hands certainly weren't eloquent enough to express my thoughts, my emotions. We fell silent. Strangely, out there amongst all of those translucent blue miles from land, the most vibrant yellow, black and white butterfly fluttered up to the boat as though, at long last, it had arrived. The young woman's surprise allowed her smile to slip through for the first time on the crossing. She cooed. I turned to watch just as the butterfly lost its inclination to land and fatally, I thought at the time, flutter out to sea. My mind grasped at fleeting things with which to make an analogy for the butterfly. The number of dead in New York returned to me, a feeling as though my seat had dropped from under me. The couple pretended not to notice my moist eyes.

I wouldn't learn the details for two more days when, returning to Bali, I found the streets buzzing with newspaper boys hawking days-old Australian papers with front pages that looked like advertisements for action thrillers—fantastic explosions, debris, victims, rescue workers. These boys were absolutely giddy with the unexpected windfall this kind of news had brought them. The disturbing earnestness of their smiles as they held up the papers fraught with images of destruction unsettled me as though each was the first slight. Soon the boys were selling four- and five-day-old papers for the amount they would have earned in a week. "America broken," one boy said smiling.

No airplanes flew in or out of the United States at that time. There were U.S. citizens stranded in foreign airports all over the world. They spent their last dollars on airport food, and they slept on benches. Although I'd been dealt a fortunate stroke to be grounded on Bali, a kind of cacophonous Hindu combination of Tijuana and Waikiki, I still felt set adrift in the South Sea. The few Americans around at the time sought out television sets with access to CNN. They could be seen huddled around tables in cafés and bars, watching and talking somberly like confederates of a terrible secret. I couldn't stand the feeling. So, I returned to G-land on the eastern tip of Java—a place, I thought, that would be sheltered from CNN, the facts, the paranoia, the emotional whirlwind.

"TOMORROW, HE'LL WANT to kill you," said a thickset Aussie surfer, feigning comedy. It was his eyes that revealed a sentiment more serious than his mouth let on. They crinkled at the edges while his mouth bent into a weak smile. This was at the shore of Alas Purwo National Park's verdant jungle in eastern Java. I'd befriended a few of the young Javanese who spent the dry season here as a kind of working vacation. At the time, I'd been joking around with a 19-year-old Muslim boy whose name I'd forgotten because everyone called him "Pussy Lover." Some admirably crass Australians taught him the phrase, and he'd taken to it as a giggling self-declaration. I called him Pussy Lover as well, and he called me *Banchong*—a transvestite particular to Balinese culture. The block-headed Aussie had caught us sharing a joke, and as we laughed, he blurted out his forecast. "Tomorrow, he'll want to kill you."

The sentence should have meant nothing.

Pussy Lover stopped laughing. A question seemed to cross his face. I did not begrudge the stupid remark because I was well aware of the news that should have remained outside the park. It filtered in and hung around our jungle camp like the rats that invaded our sleeping quarters at night. In Jakarta, for example,

a group of young Muslims reportedly stormed a few local hotels
and demanded the registry from the hotel staff. They had come,
they said, looking for Americans. The hotel staff refused their
demands, and in doing so, prompted this threat: that should the
mob return to find Americans the next day, there would be blood.
The U.S. embassy had seen demonstrations. Yet, most remarkably,
a national newspaper reported that an Indian newspaper said
Osama bin Laden was hiding in Indonesia. Indonesia's president
denied it, but the report seemed to make sense to anyone who
wanted it to. This was, after all, the most populous Muslim nation
on Earth. The hubbub caused two Americans staying in the park to
speculate that Indonesia would be bombed, and soon. I remember
the beautiful day, the clarity of the water and vibrancy of the sky,
when these two Americans fled the park in a small hired boat. As I
watched it cross the bay, I hoped the boat was big enough to carry
their paranoia with them.

It seemed to for a short time. But in its place there was an odd
sort of smugishness emitted by the remaining Australians. That
afternoon, the blockheaded Aussie surfer informed me that "the
two Americans have escaped." His tone suggested that I could
share his implication; that the fair-weather Americans who left that
day were running. In a sense, the current season of unease for the
Americans must have felt an ironic turn of events for this hardened
contingent of Australian Indo veterans. They'd been smarting since
their nation's official involvement in East Timor. Many felt they'd

been forced into conflict with their neighbor by the United States, and the conflict itself had given them a brief non grata status in Indonesia—their favorite "holiday" country to "get pissed" in, where life was "too easy" and all the good things were "a bit of the gold."

The gold at the end of that dry season on the equator was real, though. It shimmered as each evening's sunset reflected from the shallow waters covering Grajagan Bay's massive reef. It shimmered in spectra of color that seem to belong only here, only in the evenings in the dry season. Tiny elderly Javanese women wearing Chinese hats and faded scarves waded into this golden light just as they waded into the shallow waters covering the reef like a translucent film. They stooped and hunched as though burdened not only by rattan baskets loaded with the day's haul of shells, but by the delicious joy this kind of light can bring.

FROM THE WATER in the Bali Strait, the twin volcanoes of Eastern Java looked to be ethereal guardsmen, stately, unmovable, ageless. From the ferry deck, I could see both Java and Bali, so close it made me feel like stretching my arms to touch their shores. Although in perpetual jockey between them, this ferry seemed momentary, as though after we landed its rusty iron hull would melt away into the sea like a brown sugar cube into water. Under the deck, a couple dozen buses and trucks, a handful of cars and a few motorbikes lay like eggs waiting to be hatched. Ill-at-ease passengers paced the deck trying to shake the smell of diesel from their imaginations. The ferry loading had proceeded like an evacuation, but once on board, all of my travel companions seemed to have what they wanted. The large South African had his beer. Wayan was getting his sleep. An American passenger named Manuel was getting distance from the unknowable intentions of Java's Muslim population.

The streets of Bali teemed with the familiar threadbare motorbikes and wayward *bemos* and colorful foot traffic. But it was the ornamentation that told a separate story. Unlike Java, everything that moved in Bali at the time seemed to be hijacked by ceremony. Bali's Hindu families had been saving their every rupiah for this moment nearing the full moon. They'd saved only to splurge on beautifully colored ceremonies and offerings of fruit and cakes and incense and chimes and bells. The streets buzzed with traditionally dressed Balinese cutting through side streets, one arm directing a motorbike, the other cradling a chicken. Frequently, a slowly trodding motorbike was laden with an entire family in route: mamma in back sitting sidesaddle with toddler mashed between her and papa, the driver, who encaged another young child sitting on the tank with arms extended to the handlebars. All wore beautiful sarongs with bright sashes, the men and boys in white collar-less jackets and hats; women in intricately laced blouses that sprung with lovely tanned cleavage, their dark hair pinned high on their heads. All these delicate people balanced on machines weaved from side streets onto boulevards, around and between enormous industrial trucks and traffic, and back into the alleys like cackling motorized rabbits.

Disembarking from the ferry and entering this hive of purposeful pomp felt like being delivered into the emerald city. Bamboo poles dressed with woven palm ornaments marked the road. Flower pedals splashed the streets. Neighborhood temples emitted a distant clanging, bonging, tinkling music with animistic Asian timing.

But somewhere along the way I realized that this air seethed with the same perpetual odor of industrialization commingling with the fragrance of the plumeria and a meek scent of clove. The rice paddies shuddered with the same green and in the same westerly wind. I realized that the elements that made up this country were the same as those that made up Java. I thought of the declarations I heard a Balinese man make against his neighbors and countrymen just after the terrorist attacks in the United States: "Muslims no good for Bali."

Around Medewi, the sun began to sink into the haze of trash and forest fires as into a layered molten sea. The resulting incandescence illuminated everything with its powdery amber light. This light landed on ragged palms and the neighborhood temples, and also on the face of a certain elderly Balinese woman I saw walking at the side of the road. She wore a neatly arranged sarong, but no blouse. Her face, radiant in this light, was the archetype of Balinese beauty—aged only by the years, not the elements. Her gray hair was pinned in a bun behind her head. Her shoulders were slight but not bent, her arms thin and swinging, as were her bare breasts, small and still shapely. I suppose I should have been shocked to see a half-naked old lady walking down the street. But what I found shocking was my attraction to her. Her regal gait caught me. It conjured a time before this afternoon when Western missionaries had yet to influence Bali's women to hide that part of themselves— a time before industrialization and a time when foreign wars remained more foreign. Her gait and the upheld angle of her face seemed to comprise a protest. She seemed to demonstrate as best she could against the loss of her childhood paradise on Bali. This stroll became a protest against the loss of paradise, the loss of inno- cence, in the small ways regular people do—the way I did, just by seeing how it's done on the road home.

JUST OVER A year later, on October 12, 2002, Islamic militants from Java detonated two bombs in the heart of Bali's Kuta Beach, killing 202 and injuring 209 people. The bombs, set off 15 to 20 seconds apart, were designed to reek the maximum havoc and destroy the tourism infrastructure on which many Balinese depend. As of this writing, two Indonesians have been sentenced to death for their part in the bombing and one has been sentenced to life in prison. The mastermind of the attacks is not known.

Hills Like One Thousand Dead Dinosaurs

WE WERE TOLD quite specifically not to come here. If we did, we were admonished to drive only on the main freeway, the spacious N2, and even then, not to stop anywhere in the Transkei except for the well-lit Shell Ultra stations, which appear out of the rural blanket like mini chapters of the Las Vegas strip. While still in Cape Town, we were threatened with parables: those people who have stopped out of compassion, or ignorance, have been robbed, raped and burned. The burning is a constant theme, whether in the rural Homelands or in South Africa's townships. Burning seemed to possess the cultural facsimile of a pair of cement shoes in the United States—a brutal death as well as a disposal of the evidence.

To this end, Henry acted out a surprise attack, his forearm extending downward and wrist bent inward to conceal a "rod or a knife," as he explained with a thick Afrikaner accent. This was in the living room of a 100-year-old Victorian guest house in the Cape Town neighborhood of Sea Point. Henry, a thin chinless man of Dutch decent in his late 30s, was a frequent resident of the guest house. (Although, when we first arrived, I assumed from the way he spoke to the "coloured" ladies who ran the place that he owned it. But, no, said Katie, the head of the house, he is only a dolt who is friendly with the owner.) Henry had said that he was a policeman under the former government and, toward the changeover, a volunteer paramilitary in a group that attempted a coup against Mandela's government. He and many others, Henry said, felt betrayed by F. W. de Klerk, the former president who is partly credited with disassembling apartheid, as well as his own regime.

When Henry discovered that my girlfriend and I planned to take the coastal route from Cape Town to Durban, immediately he sat down to draw a map that virtually circumnavigated the Transkei. "After you have done your surfing at Jeffery's Bay, you will rise at 4 a.m. and you will drive without stopping until you reach Durban." On the map he circled the entire southeastern corner of the country. In fact, he circled what was nearly its own country. One of four homelands to gain "nominal" independence in the '60s under the former government, the Transkei was once again consumed by the New South Africa in 1994. "There are Xhosa and Zulu there," Henry said, "and they are very aggressive. Very aggressive!"

I planned to do as I pleased. But over the next few days of our preparations in Cape Town, initially amiable Henry became more disturbed by our plan. First he suggested we fly to Durban. Then, as in a fit of enlightenment, he suggested we take the Baz Bus, a backpacker's bus that follows a similar route and stops at hostels and guest houses along the way. "You will be with your own people," he said excitedly. "British and European." But, I pointed out, we'd already obtained a fine set of wheels. And I'd already been jerking up and down Sea Point's San Francisco–like hills teaching myself how to shift with my left hand and how to make the complicated right-hand turns. It was about this time that Henry cornered us in the dark wood-trimmed living room of Ashby House with dire stories of lawlessness and an impromptu lesson in hand-to-hand combat.

ANYWHERE ELSE, THIS would have been called "drive-by tourism." But in the Transkei, the road is the experience. It is the river that draws its people from the vastness of their blond, endlessly rolling hills. It is the means of communication, the market, the stockyard, the athletics club, the hangout, the day-care center. Nothing is hidden from it. And it's easy to see, smell and feel along this meandering and swaybacked stretch that there is no human transaction too sacrosanct for a paved road.

The hills roll and jostle like the hides of dead dinosaurs bleaching in the sun. They are intermittently tan and brown. There are no trees, no bushes and few fences. The brush that colors the landscape is bald in patches, ruffled in others and holds an uncanny resemblance to the mangy coats of the roadside dogs. Every great now and again among the varied tones of decomposition are tiny patches of emerald green—gardens that appear through distance as spots of brilliant color—as conspicuous here as they would be on the moon.

The most bizarre protrusions from the smooth, undulating

landscape are these clusters of mud and dung randavels. They are as perfectly round as tin cans and mounted by thatch roofs peaked like Chinese hats. At the pinnacle of each thick, funnel-shaped roof sits a spent car tire. Many of these are filled with concrete and decorated by shards of colored glass sparkling in the broad, thin sunlight. These particular randavels are painted what my copilot Michelle contends is a sea-foam green—although in other parts of the Transkei they are white. Curiously though, none of the backs of the mud homes are covered in paint. Often a cluster of homes will be accompanied by a rectangular structure with mud walls that resemble Play-Doh slab construction. Corrugated tin covers these cousins with corners, and the metal is held down from the elements by bricks, rocks and more spent tires. The homesteads are spaced as distantly as homes on the prairie, and the overall effect is as striking as if we'd driven out to the Midwest only to discover people living in teepees and buffalo roaming among the tall grass.

The great unifier is the dome of sky, clear and seamless; its sheer size constituting a palpable weight. Randavels, vehicles and the road itself are all diminished in its presence. A hill rises and we follow its incline, asserting our only power here: speed. And at the hill's apex we glimpse a ribbon of darker blue farther out on the horizon where the sky would logically continue its embrace of the earth. We see the opaque blue of the greater sky sinking into this darker blue. Then the hill we're on peaks and we disappear into its blondness again. The road continues, and I have only the vaguest idea that what I've just seen is one of the meanest corners of the Indian Ocean.

But at the moment I'm considering the word "secondary" and what it means to map reading. According to the map, a secondary road can be paved or not, grated or not: it can dog leg or dead end without indication on the map. What it can't be in this country, where a place does not exist without a road, is lightly traveled. The one I'm driving on is one lane, mined with potholes and littered with abysmal craters. At times staggered and avoidable, there are those potholes that seem to have consumed this stretch of asphalt some time in the Mesozoic era. To avoid the potholes I swerve into oncoming lanes. Yet, so do trucks, big and small, as well as minibuses—those harbingers of the modern African death. There is an entire politics of potholes and lane poaching. I begin to understand that these politics directly relate to the size of your vehicle. Ours is small, so I learn also that it is acceptable for a trucker to risk my life—and his—to miss whatever absence of asphalt he wishes. This is a realization that came head on about the time a cackling tanker of a truck with the maintenance record of one of these roadside bovine veers into my lane. Its appearance gives me reason to doubt my position, as I had just recently taught myself how to drive on the right-hand side of the car and the left-hand side of the road. The trucker's confidence in his rights sets me reeling inside, while I hold a line and thread the needle between the trucker, the potholes and a dog on the shoulder.

After this, I decide simply to take the jarring. I don't own the car. And in any case, the oncoming traffic isn't always incased in metal. Often it's a goat or a cow or a small child whose head is half the size of his body. I see a particularly big hole coming on; I see all of the soft squishy things I could kill; I brace myself against the steering wheel; I tighten my kidneys, and then I can taste the bang like a metallic lightening bolt in my teeth. After several of these, I begin to swerve among the divots within my lane. It takes a certain kind of eloquence. In a daze of passing kilometers, I begin to suspect the positioning of the potholes is not senseless, does not exist in chaos, but that each communicates in a kind of Morse code. And I believe I know now what they were saying. They read, dot dot, "Get off the fucking road before you die here."

Instead of laughing when we soon learn that the Transport Minister of South Africa has been caught driving with a fake driver's license, we only note the tragic believability of it.

MICHELLE, AT 24, is petite and blonde with a small easily smiling mouth and blue eyes as clear as that distant Indian Ocean. Until recently she'd never been outside of her native California. She looks out the window at this Spartan place with a Podunk excitement. She laughs lightly at the Xhosa woman walking along the side of the road with a purse stacked on her head and her arms swinging freely at her sides. So far, we've seen women with bundles of sticks, gallon jugs of water and wire fencing balanced on their heads. But it is a woman a few kilometers ahead who marches vigilantly with a backpack stacked on her head, its arm straps flapping in the wind, who encourages Michelle to yell out the window with the most sincere effort, "That goes on your back." Michelle points at her own and reiterates, "The back." The Xhosa woman offers the look of someone who knows a freak when she sees one, especially a misplaced white girl hanging out the side of Volkswagen. Who takes fashion tips from passersby anyway? A group of boys appears at the side of the road, running in our direction. Their faces are painted ceremonial white, one like a mask, another like a raccoon's. They run like boys just out of church. One of the boys drags a branch behind him. It is senseless to us, and they are happy.

But there are other sights that bring Michelle consternation. One is a dead mule half in the road being pecked apart by a dog mindless of the traffic. I swerve to miss it, knowing full well the next vehicle won't. We'd seen several dead dogs, but here we are minutes short of seeing a dead dog on top of a dead mule. Then we pass a minibus crashed into a ditch at the side of the road. Its evacuated passengers stand circling it. They view the minibus in the same way we would have regarded that dead mule—had we pulled over and shooed the dog away, as Michelle suggested.

A few days earlier, driving on the loopy and intermittently paved R61 through more endlessly golden rolling hills, we come to a hub of activity the map calls Flagstaff. There are more people in the road than vehicles. The town seems to be a short strip of dilapidated European block buildings. Yet, in this downtown, all of the selling is going on outside. Everything is for sale: worn basketball shoes, used T-shirts, oranges, bags of cement, sides of beef hanging openly in the dusty street. Women in big skirts and colorful head wraps hold dominion over blankets displaying their goods. I spot one woman with a green headdress unsuccessfully attempting to tend her customers and defend her cabbages from a marauding goat. She bargains with a customer, the goat nabs a big head of cabbage and she turns back in time only to swat the goat in the ass as it makes off. Although technically it's a highway, we come to a point in this marketplace where we cannot move our small car forward or backward. We are engulfed in people, and they are looking at us like curiosities brought in as the market's entertainment. These are stares unaccustomed to discretion, probing and unrelenting. "This is Africa," I say wistfully, and Michelle, staring and being stared at, agrees: "This is Africa." We inch forward, the street continues crowded, dusty and hot. Still, there are open blazes going on in the midst of it. They reek of burning plastic. In the bluish orange flames we can distinguish metal springs and other trash traditionally considered unburnable. Everything is being sold, everything is being burned. The entire sense of the event comes into focus for Michelle and she announces with resolve, like a new believer in the faith, "If you can't sell it, burn it."

As the crowd thins and we make our way out of Flagstaff, we find large groups of children walking toward the market. In a group of teenage boys, I see the first white face in two days of traveling in the Transkei, and given the paranoia of Europeans in South Africa these days, I find the sight of him gripping. The boy wears glasses and is dressed like his colleagues in tennis shoes and khaki pants. He has an ease to his gait. Not until we are right upside the boys do I notice the tight curl of his distinctly yellow hair and the paleness of his eyes: he is an albino. And I know right then, my captured attention to him, says more about me than it does the place.

We come to a tee at the end of town and turn left on a whim. Outside town we once again enter the roll and sway of a landscape as varied and uneven as an old hyena's back. Somewhere among the merging of all these middle tones of wheat, we come upon another group of children laughing expectantly at the side of the road. The pavement, for 20 yards, is splattered with orange peels and pulp. As we advance, three of the children bowl rotten oranges into the road, hoping to watch them smashed by our tires. In the rearview mirror I see them laughing and cheering.

Ironically, an hour later I pull over to buy some oranges from a young woman who has washed and stacked hers like prized jewels on top of a cardboard box. She sits 10 feet from the road. In front of her is one of this road's few signs, a painted sheet of plywood that's fallen down, one corner resting in the dirt. The sign reads: "National Department of Public Works, Together Fighting Poverty." I buy two oranges and then take a photo of her. She smiles. From a small collection of mud randavels behind us comes a cackling crew of kids. They are on me fast and they want their photos taken, too. So I take a shot and, immediately, one says, "Gib us mawney." A straggling little latecomer approaches yelling, "Mawney, mawney!"

ABOUT A MONTH later on the porch of a family-run lodge overlooking the final green bend of a river, its sandy mouth and the blue of the Indian Ocean, I find myself thinking about the Zambezi sharks that have been known to swim as far as 10 kilometers up river and nab full grown cattle wading at the river banks. This is in Cinsta, just a few kilometers short of the Kei River's mouth and the southern edge of the Transkei. Technically, it is the land that is called the "Wild Coast," wooded thickets, rock cliffs, reefs of volcanic rock and sand beaches, but it is the ocean that is terrifying. This piece of water is one of the most shark-infested corners of the globe. There are surf breaks near here, where surfers are picked off with a certain regularity. Ten kilometers farther out in the Indian is the Mozambique current, which generates massive swells that run parallel to the continent. It is a shipwreck alley, where ships have high-sided between two peaks in one of these swells, leaving the vessel's own weight to break it in half. Shipwrecks were responsible for the area's very first contacts with Europeans. And at least two towns on the coast are named after shipwrecks: Port St. Johns after the 1552 wreck of the *São João*, which forced its survivors to then walk to Mozambique, and

Coffee Bay, named after a wreck in 1863 that supposedly left a mess of coffee beans on the beach.

Here on the Cinsta porch, though, the sun is warm and the view imposing. I sit down to a picnic table with a Zulu man named Philip. At least, he says, Philip is the closest approximation to his Zulu name. He looks to be about 40. His skin is very dark, except for curious, almost ceremonial-looking vertical scars on his cheeks and forehead. His hair is clipped close to his head. He speaks slowly, at low volume, and I must listen closely to sort out the words. Philip is stranded here at the moment, he says. Then, after a few empty seconds, he reluctantly confides the story of the previous night when a vehicle belonging to one of his colleagues mysteriously ran off the dirt track and flipped. Philip is slow to let on that he is the driver responsible for the crash. Although he doesn't admit it, it seems as though he'd fallen asleep behind the wheel. Sighing inter-mittently, he drops his head, shamefaced. But, in fact, he is lucky. The mortality rate along the Transkei's roads is ridiculously high for both drivers and pedestrians, as well as for livestock. He and his passenger are unhurt. Also, the staff of the lodge is arranging a recovery effort for the vehicle.

Meanwhile, we eat a simple breakfast made by ladies from neighboring Xhosa villages. I discover that Philip's job requires him to drive to every corner of the Transkei. A former local politician involved with the African National Congress, he now works for a nonprofit organization dedicated to community tourism development. Philip meets with chiefs and tribal elders to encourage native communities to develop their own low impact tourism infrastructure. The lodge we're at now is one of the most efficiently run and most popular of its kind on the coast. It is owned by a family with deep roots in the community and a portion of their profit pays for a local school. Still, the family is white, and the natives are employees. Philip believes that creating a native-owned tourism infrastructure will keep the large hotels and golf courses out and the Wild Coast pristine.

We talk of the difficulty of traveling from one town on this coast to the next. It's necessary to drive an hour or two to a main north/south highway and then take another secondary or dirt road a few more hours back to the coast. This to cover a distance that might take 40 minutes on a legitimate sealed road spanning the distance between towns. So, I suggest one, and then without thinking it through, I add, "Like the Pacific Coast Highway in California."

"Yes," says Philip. "Some people wish to destroy the Wild Coast." And, the point is a blunt one, a coastal road would.

I tell Philip rather plainly the warnings I received in Cape Town. Who could forget roadside rapes and the burnings? "There was one incident in 1992," Philip says wearily. "And because of 'old politics' they keep this rumor going." Patiently, as though to a child, he explains that because the area was a homeland, because it is the birthplace of Nelson Mandela, Winnie Mandela and current President Thabo Mbeki, as well as a stronghold of the ANC, the "old establishment" has campaigned against it. And, if this is true, they've done it rather successfully.

COFFEE BAY IS a beautiful little W carved out of the raw coast. A wooded hillock juts up and out, pronouncing the point between its two scooped bays. A tidal river empties out into the first, and the second extends to a half-moon of white sandy beach with a right-hand pointbreak on its southern end. Until reaching Coffee Bay, the amber hills of the Transkei would seem to roll right up to the sea without a sliver of green to acknowledge the water's existence. But the green is here, hidden. I realize this as we step out of the car onto chalky dirt before a tidal rivermouth. The river and its entry to the sea is lined by foliage. The tide is up and the murky thing is flowing out. Instead of the scent of pastures, we now smell the ocean. We can see the backpacker hostels, made up of randavels and a central house, on the far bank of the river. There is no way our little car could forge the river as shallow as it is. So, Michelle decides to skip across river rocks to the other side and see about a room.

As soon as she's gone, I am confronted by three boys, each one smaller than the next. Spaced from each other even, they stare at me in silence and remain 10 feet away. Their faces are angular, their eyes big. One has a shaved head, another's spindly hair has formed little lent-like balls, another's is a short foam core. Only one of them wears shoes; they all wear T-shirts. I retrieve an orange from the car, peel it and offer slices to the boys. Each one steps forward in turn, accepts a slice and then steps back three paces. We eat our slices and reflect on the river. Then the tallest boy says, "You need a guide to Hole in the Wall. I take you." He means an arch carved from a cliff a short hike away.

"No," I say, "I'll wait."

"You go fishing, I take you."

"No, thank you."

"You buy ganja, I go get."

"Weed," interrupts the smaller boy. I can see his spiky little teeth.

"No, thanks."

"Gib me mawney," resumes the tallest boy.

"Mawney," the smallest boy adds.

"Shouldn't you boys be in school?" I ask, wondering if there is a school.

"School vacations," says the tallest boy. I look to the smallest boy, and he shows me his little teeth again. We wait in silence, and I think through the aspects of begging and dope dealing on school holidays. Then Michelle returns.

THE BACKPACKER HOSTELS—there are two side by side—have a buzz about them. There are young international travelers taking in the sun, and there is talk of walking to Hole in the Wall, fishing, surfing, swimming and collecting seashells. But most laze around, eat or read. Some of them are Peace Corps or foreign teacher volunteers on leave. Most are just "traveling." Just about all of them have taken the Baz Bus to the Shell Ultra station in Umtata where they were retrieved by valiant drivers from the hostels' staff. A select few have hiked here along the Wild Coast, camping and staying in randavels, some from St. Johns, and some from farther. They all have stories about what they've seen.

We choose one of the hostels because of its traditional randavels. The clapboard before the gate reads: "Space Cakes, Shakes, Coffee & Tea." So we learn also that the travelers are getting terribly, and openly, stoned. And this might explain the number of travelers doing nothing on the sunny day we arrived.

While getting our first meal (an awful chicken concoction made by a Swedish girl), I overhear the proprietor's tirade on the difficulty of maintaining the space cakes and everything else. He is a middle-aged South African with leathery skin and a shock of graying hair. Youthful in movement, though, he speaks quickly with a pronounced accent. His wife is a Dutch woman, about 30, who came to the Transkei as a visitor and never left. The two of them are juggling their one-year-old son, as well as their duties, because today they are making the pilgrimage to Umtata and are attempting to ready the staff for their absence. "You must wrap the leftover space cakes in plastic before you throw them out. And also, you must make certain the rubbish lid is weighted down," he says to the Swedish girl behind the kitchen counter. He sits down across from Michelle and me and sits his son in his lap and begins to feed him.

"Last time we went away, the dogs got into the rubbish and ate all of the space cake," he says. "We thought they had a terrible case of rabies. The disease is very bad here. All four of them were acting like spastics. They ran around extremely paranoid and would not come near us. We were terribly frightened for them, so we drove the dogs to the veterinarian in Umtata. But while waiting in the clinic several hours later, we noticed they'd calmed down quite a lot. Then we realized that they must have been absolutely stoned from eating space cakes." He chuckles like a wily old cowboy.

I notice a sign before walking out the gate on the way to the beach. It reads: "If you want to buy ganja, please consult with one of the staff so that we can obtain the correct price as well as ensure quality." Outside the gate, I meet the first three friends I made in Coffee Bay. "Walk to Hole in the Wall," the spindly haired one says, and I wonder if he remembers our earlier conversation. "Go fishing? Buy weed?"

I have a surfboard under my arm and I'm wearing trunks with no pockets, still, they follow for a short while until they spot other prospects. I wade through the murky tidal river before I get to the beach proper. The ocean water is the most beautiful deep blue, with black boulders set in the shallows. The beach is empty except for a couple of boys on its far side. These boys are huddled around something. When I reach them, I realize that they are a pit crew working on one of their handmade wire trucks. The trucks are ingeniously made. Wire stolen from cattle fencing forms the frame, mono-shock suspension and axles. Copper wire stolen from downed telephone cable binds the larger wire in place at its joints and aluminum cans, chopped and spliced together, make the wheels. A steering column attached to the front axle rises out of the cab of each truck so that the crude steering wheel sits chest level to each of the small drivers. The boys with sandy feet and dirty T-shirts are apprehensive of me. But the 12-year-old head mechanic, Adrian, allows me to take his truck for a test drive. The wheels turn nicely, the handling is impeccable. Divots in the sand are no obstacle for the homemade suspension, and before I realize it, I'm running down the beach as fast as I can and the truck before me is weightless. Soon enough, we are all racing trucks. We are turning and peeling out, we're doing doughnuts and hill climbs. We've forgotten about the Transkei's roads, the camel's hump of a hill behind us or the crash of waves before us. We're running, we're driving, we're free.

At least this is the way Michelle found me when she came sometime later to retrieve me from the ocean. And I am a proud fellow truck driver when the boys refuse to let me go just yet.

A few days later I pack away my very own wire truck, sold to me by Adrian who shrugs and lies a little when he says it only took him a half-hour to make and insists that I take extra spares—"You will need them in America." This time Michelle is driving as we move on, back into the herd of dead dinosaurs that make up Transkei's "Wild Interior."

THE ROAD AND the rules of friction have let go of us. Our brakes are locked and we are sliding ferociously forward. Michelle's arms are seized pistons against the steering wheel. Through the windshield an insignificant death approaches us with speed in the form of a rattletrap pickup whose missing grill is open like a black maw. It has emerged around a blind corner in our lane, the left lane. It does not budge or slow. Michelle, against her best American intuition, does not swerve right. What she has done is apply the weight of the Hoover Dam to the brake pedal and its hydraulics release our hold on the road. We are floating forward, and already I can see the small article in the back of the Sunday *Times*, and the red tape of the embassy and the difficulty our families will have getting our bodies home.

Suddenly our tires bite the pavement again. Our car stops hard. It dies. And the grim reaper behind the glare of the pickup's windshield turns left just slightly, just enough to absolutely slaughter us had Michelle hinted right. The vehicle careens by us so closely that Michelle could have stuck her head out and kissed the pane of glass next to the driver's head. But the pickup is gone over a hill as fast as it came. And we are left there stalled safely. I understand we are free to go on. But we can't just yet, Michelle and I. We simply sit on the road in the silence of the tall grasses and stare expectantly at the road ahead.

Tahiti Iti

FOR A SPLIT second I imagined I was surfing with one of the tawny-skinned girls from Gauguin's early paintings. Seventeen-year-old Hena, brown-eyed and flawless, bobbed in the warm sea water with a timeless Polynesian grace. Around her, young and old Tahitians entertained themselves on just about anything that floated. At their backs lay a black-sand beach, a palm-shrouded river-mouth and a dramatic blue-green valley peaking on either side with jagged volcanic spires. This must have been what Captain Cook saw in 1776 when he dropped anchor in Matavai Bay and recorded the sight of Tahitians canoe-surfing the little beach inside of Point Venus. Yet this was 2003. Hena had memorized every Avril Lavigne lyric, could recite lines from her favorite movie *Blue Crush* and had just paddled out on a modern longboard. Still, it was the happy-go-lucky way she did it that caught my eye.

This is where Tahiti surfs, in the average, sloppy beachbreaks. Papara Beach, in particular, is where '80s World Championship Tour competitor Vetea "Poto" David brings his kids, where Tahitian flight attendants and hotel workers surf on their days off and where Hira Teriinatoofa, the island's only representative on the World Qualifying Series, sharpens his beachbreak skills. The waves that draw foreign surfers and media attention—the waves that have come to define the surfer's image of Tahiti—are often too labor intensive for a quick go out. Most of them are a 20-minute paddle from the beach, requiring a boat or a strong desire to reach them. The first is an expensive luxury on an island with one of the highest costs of living in the world. So the average Tahitian surfer often settles for convenience.

"I was used to surfing shitty waves," Poto says of his early preparation for the WCT. "People ask why I wasn't surfing Teahupoo in the early '80s. I was a kid, and I didn't have a car to go searching for waves, or money for gas."

Considering the importance of the sand banks off Papara Beach to the development of Tahiti's young surfers, the lack of aggressive competition in the water that day approached mysterious. Waves were shared, and the hierarchy didn't discriminate between canoe, surfboard or bodyboard. It was lighthearted in a truly Polynesian way, and more than the warm water or the volcanic mountains in the background, it was the free atmosphere that distinguished it from a crowded, sloppy beachbreak anywhere else.

A FEW HUNDRED yards away, 28-year-old Raimana van Bastolear sat in his modest house, occasionally peering through the open door to the action down at the rivermouth. He hadn't surfed in days, and the 3-foot conditions didn't inspire him. This was February and he said he'd rather wait the month or two before Teahupoo began breaking properly. It seemed that a surf would do him some good.

A beautiful day had unfolded, and he'd been shut up inside.
Because he is trilingual and has developed contacts across the
Pacific, his surfing career has evolved into a kind of ambassadorship
of Tahitian surfing. There were arrangements to be made for visiting pros, equipment to be maintained and he'd been hired to lay
the groundwork for a reality TV show to be produced on the
island. But his role as ambassador had him surrounded by papers
and to-do lists. Their details, it seemed, had greased his slide into
an ambivalent funk.

"We told them this was our day," he said, recounting an alterca-
tion out at Teahupoo during the previous season. "We towed a few
foreigners. And they fucked us. They fucked us."

An international pro, Otto Flores of Puerto Rico, made the
cover of *Surfer* on a wave Raimana towed him into. This wasn't
unforeseen, but during that session, Raimana demanded to those
present that a Tahitian surfer bag a cover shot. It was their wave,
and their ski, after all. For Raimana, the demand seemed reason-
able, if not overdue. But demands made in the water don't travel
well, and the sentiment never made it off the island. A sense of
betrayal lingered in the story. Along with Bgarn and Manoa
Drollet, Raimana believed he helped introduce Teahupoo to the
world. Now, the beast was a free-for-all.

"You have to be over there [Teahupoo] when it's big to understand what's going on. It's no good talking about it," Raimana said
dismissively to me, a journalist from the same publication he felt

had slighted him. Yet I knew it takes more than being here to understand the gripe completely. You'd have to be a Tahitian surfer with an eye on the prize.

"Things changed like that," said Teriinatoofa snapping his fingers. "I think Teahupoo is bringing more of everything to Tahiti." Without any serious heritage in the competitive realm, with the Gotcha Pro in 1998 the island became the site of the WCT's most harrowing event. And socially indicative, a Tahitian wave replaced Pipeline's 30-year reign on the plastered walls of surf culture. Yet the surfers at the source, the ones who helped midwife that wave into the world consciousness, are left wondering what this increase of "everything" means for them. They see the surfers who devote themselves to Pipeline garnering salaries, while the surfers who devote themselves to Teahupoo make a few extra bucks in May when the WCT creates a few off-stage jobs.

"It's fucked up now," Poto admitted, "because people want to make a living out of it." Like John Steinbeck's novel *The Pearl*, in which a young fisherman discovers "the pearl of the world," but soon finds his simple life destroyed by the greed it inspires, the Tahitian surfers knew they'd discovered something of great value, but weren't necessarily prepared for its consequences. What are those consequences? Localism, rifts over proprietorship, economic disputes, unwanted development and unrequited ambitions. Poto surmised the situation with an honest bluntness: "The good comes with the bad."

Despite his funk that day, Raimana's accomplishment in this arena has been a hard-earned example of "the good." He was 20 before giving up bodyboarding for surfing. But almost as soon as he could stand on a board, he was getting barreled, and his first published photo was taken only a couple months into his surfing life. Only a few years ago Raimana was training to become a flight attendant. Yet with the first contest held at Teahupoo, a WQS event in 1997, Raimana foresaw the benefits to come. Since then he has expanded his career in surfing to include water-safety skills and big-wave expertise. But, like most recent gains in Tahitian surfing, his are irrevocably linked to just one wave. At that moment, it seemed a bit like living in a one-factory town.

"For me and Manoa, it's Teahupoo. That's how we make our living. Period. When I realized I could make money [by surfing], I knew I had to surf the big waves and get barreled," he said.

Just then, Hena, who works as a cook and maid for Raimana, carried her dripping longboard into the backyard and set it next to the canoe and fishing gear—all water sports are integral in Tahitian life. When she entered the small house with a quiet satisfaction, I realized the divide between her and Raimana's take on surfing marked a change in the times. I found myself wondering how the business of Teahupoo and the influence of the foreigners who come to surf it will affect Hena and her friends down at the rivermouth.

A few minutes later, checking the surf from his doorstep, Raimana spotted Poto down at the beach. There had been a dispute between them. It seems the island isn't big enough for two full-time surf ambassadors. And currently, the two local heroes of Teahupoo weren't on speaking terms. Raimana definitely wouldn't be going for a surf now that Poto was out.

"THAT'S ALL I'VE got. Pictures," said Henry Lucas. A tan, healthy 53-year-old with dark wavy hair, Henry looked much too young to be the first modern Tahitian surfer. The Society Islands' surf culture is not historically minded. At the start of our search for the pioneers of Tahitian surfing, Raimana pointed out there are no old 16mm films, no magazines and he hadn't seen any of the old photos. So, when Raimana and I tapped Tahiti's coconut pipeline in an effort to uncover the island's oldest surfers, we had no idea the pioneers were living and surfing with everyone else. But in finding guys like Henry Lucas and Patrick Juventin, the first full-time shaper in Tahiti, we discovered a historical treasure much more engaging than a strip of celluloid film.

Still, Henry treats his place in the reemergence of Tahitian surfing as incidental. He's kept nothing of those early days but a handful of faded black and whites. In one of them, he pointed to a group of young guys leaning against cars clutching longboards. With a backdrop of palms, the photo could have been one of hundreds from Hawaii in the early '60s. Here though, it's a rare document. "That's when we started the Tahitian Surf Club," Henry said plainly.

Like Henry's unadorned speech, the word "club" is an

understatement. Formally organized in 1967, this crew's geographic isolation sparked an aggressive search for information and technique that would be more characteristic of an ancient exploration society. They taught themselves how to shape with hand planers, organized fact-finding missions to Hawaii, traveled to competitions in France and invited anyone with a knowledge of surfing to Tahiti. At one point Henry sold his house to buy a catamaran he used to explore the outer reefs. When the boat tariffs became too expensive, he dabbled in the first surf charters.

The irony is, having grown up in the South Pacific, Henry's first contact with surfing occurred in the '50s, when he was shipped off to a Santa Ana, California, boarding school. During that time a school friend who'd previously dressed like a "greaser," sporting chinos and slicked-back hair, declared one day he'd "turned surfer." The two of them started hitching rides to Newport Beach. They shared a board, slept on the sand and collected bottles for redemption value. When Henry returned to Tahiti at 13, he ferreted out the island's only surfboard. It belonged to a Frenchman who brought it to the island as a curiosity piece. Henry borrowed, surfed and destroyed the thing within a year.

So, in 1964 when Bruce Brown and the crew of the *Endless Summer* paddled out at Ins and Outs, Henry, the only kid on the island who knew what to do with a surfboard, crouched on the beach waiting for Robert August or Mike Hynson's board to wash up. Eventually, one of them did. Henry scrambled for it and poached a few waves before the board was demanded back. This event was the beginning of a cross-Pacific friendship, an exchange as monumental as those of the early explorers at Matavai Bay. Henry would soon convince his father to order 20 surfboards from California to sell in his general store. These would become the nucleus of the Tahitian Surf Club, which in turn, would build a foundation for the roughly 2,500 surfers in French Polynesia today.

Considering what lay off shore, there's a moment in Henry's youth that rivals the *Endless Summer*'s visit in importance. It was the first day the local crew was inspired to leave the beach and paddle for the distant reef pass at Ta'apuna. "It [the wave] was hairy for us," Henry said. "And then, we liked it."

In the '60s surfing shallow reef passes was not an obvious idea. Bruce Brown would come and go that first trip, without realizing the island's potential. Unlike Hawaii, where a range of reef breaks sits close to shore, Tahiti's barrier reefs stretch for unbroken miles like a submerged sidewalk. There are relatively few reef passes and only a handful of them are surfed consistently. The day the local boys decided to search for something new began as fluke and ended with a leap of faith.

"I will always remember that day [when they first surfed Ta'apuna]. We were five boys. We were young and we didn't have a license to drive," reminisced Patrick Juventin with his classic French Polynesian accent. Though he was just a grommet when he and some friends rallied Henry—the elder statesman by then—to drive them around the island to look for waves, Patrick would become the island's first real surfboard innovator, shaper and glasser.

Imagine the reef at Ta'apuna: it's a sharp, visible slab sitting just under the water's surface. The wave is fast and unforgiving. The boys were shaping their own boards by then, and these pigs were a bit rough even for the late '60s. They had no leashes, and the water in the channel would have been pushing out toward the island of Moorea looming to the west. But the experience was a kick in the ass. "We think, wow, incredible and we surf [there] the next Saturday and every week after that," said Patrick.

Today, when Ta'apuna is working, there will be scores of surfers from Papeete and the southern districts scrapping for sets and crumbs alike. There will be boats in the channel and a hierarchy in the lineup. The boys' first paddle out to Ta'apuna enlarged the scope of Tahitian surfing, and arguably, it was the very beginning of an outward expansion that would lead to the Tuamotus, Leeward Islands and Marquesas.

When I asked Patrick, now in his late 40s but still wearing the grin of the boy who first surfed Ta'apuna, what he thought of surfing's place in Tahiti today, he said, "It's too big, but it has to be this way, *non*? It's progress."

BOTH WQS CONTENDER Hira Teriinatoofa and I knew the waves would be junk, and we drove out to the north side to surf the beaches around Papenoo anyway. As an American expatriot I met at

Papara Beach told me rather bluntly, "The magazines love to pro-mote fantasy. Which is fine, except for...reality."

The reality is that even in paradise, conditions aren't always ideal. But Hira, 23, could find somewhere to surf just about every day. His determination is not a Tahitian trait, and I wondered where he'd picked it up as we passed through Papeete's vibrant streets. Taking odd jobs to supplement his travel budget, as well as surfing twice a day, Hira was working as hard as any Brazilian on the WQS. And as Tahiti's sole international competitor, he was doing it alone. "The hardest thing is to get out of here," he said. "Then the life on the [WQS] tour is hard, too. If you don't love the adventure, better stay home."

Even on a short stay here, you'll quickly realize that Polynesian culture is mud thick, even on Tahiti, the most urban of the Society Islands. You'll see a brawny man search a bush for the perfect flower to adorn his ear. Others will sit by the road lazily strumming ukuleles. Hip-hop fans carry their Discmans in woven palm frond baskets. And young and old seem to be perpetually traveling to or from a canoe race or practice, paddles in hand.

But it's the easy life and culture that can be most constricting to the young competitor. Hira said he's seen some of Tahiti's best surfers languish after spurts of success in the local competition scene. Some former competitors his age have families already and can't travel. Others are afraid to fly, or don't like cold water, or have lost their competitive drive to the simple daily life. Raimana said that their distance from the centers of the surf industry create tremendous obstacles in gaining decent sponsorship. As a result of these things, Tahiti seems to produce successful competitive surfers one at a time, linked together like pearls on a string.

Although Henry, Patrick and others from the original Tahitian Surf Club traveled to France and Hawaii, their protégé Arsene Harehoe was the first young competitor to travel widely to England, Japan, Puerto Rico and Australia. In 1977 Arsene, just 16, traveled to Hawaii for the first time and won "best tube" at the Smirnoff. When Hira spoke of Arsene, the word "legend" popped up frequently because, as he said, "Each time anything important has happened in Tahitian surfing, Arsene was there."

Today, Arsene is still in impeccable physical shape. When I met up with him at the shore inside of Ta'apuna, he'd just gone for a swim. Walking along shirtless, he began to imagine his paddle strokes for an upcoming canoe race. He made his hands into paddles and brushed his arms in an "S" pattern to his side. Then he stopped at a bush and found a flower for his ear. I asked him why others call him a legend, and he was characteristically modest. "Maybe because I was the only guy to do something in the surf. But probably just because I teach [the younger generation] to surf."

More than teaching the kids, Arsene shapes their boards, surfs big Teahupoo, works water safety at the big events and, of course, races canoes. But importantly, by example he showed the surfers who followed, like Poto, Heifara Tahutini and now Hira, that basing a competitive career out of Tahiti could be done. This could prove to be a critical quality, considering all that the WCT event at Teahupoo brings to Tahiti, and the growing number of local competitions it has inspired.

As Hira said, "I think Teahupoo has the people thinking more about surfing. Before it would have been soccer or canoe. There are more kids surfing because of it."

TO SIT ON the beach and listen to tales about the outer islands is like sitting in the original *Star Wars* outpost bar, absorbing fables of distant, sparkling planets. Tahiti is undeniably like the Hawaiian chain—the wafting fragrance, the volcanic earth, the dark green heights, the clouds stuck on its crown. But whereas Hawaii is established in the world's view, the number of islands in its chain counted and finite; for the industrialized world, Tahiti remains the romantic notion embedded in Gauguin's brushwork. Today its traffic jams and crowded lineups dispel the myth. But when looking at detailed maps of French Polynesia, and the number of islands and atolls seemingly caught in Tahiti's gravitational pull, the myth lingers in the imagination. Considering that Teahupoo, in clear view at the end of the only coastal road, wasn't exposed until the mid-'90s, the idea of the reef, wind and swell possibilities still undiscovered in the Society Islands blows through the mind like the restless trade winds.

In Papeete I was introduced to a twenty-something Tahitian

pearl farmer from the Tuamotus, a remote group of atolls to the north. He came to the city looking for a little fun and to buy a supply of surfboards to take back to his favorite home break. It was a story out of the American Midwest: he'd come in from the farm to the big city. Yet his farm was an aquatic one, and the "big city" was just a gathering of lights in the South Pacific.

With a knowing smirk, Poto confirmed that despite the relatively new desire for recognition on the part of Tahitian surfers, there are many surfers, especially in the outer islands, who "don't give a shit about a photographer."

They've seen what's happened at Ta'apuna, and there seems to be a weary eye on the future of Teahupoo. The result is what Poto called the "Tahitian tax," a euphemism for unfriendly lineups. Tahitians who work on surf charters will tell tales of nasty clashes between outer islanders and their charter customers. Like Steinbeck's Kino and the men who came for his "pearl of the world," for locals an approaching boatload of pros and photographers raises the "Song of the Enemy." It is a conflict certain to come to a crisis. French Polynesia has very few exports, and the fantasy wave is almost certain to become a major one. Yet, for now, Tahitians who have traveled throughout French Polynesia offer simple advise. When I'd planned a trip to Huahine, a man covered with traditional tattoos advised me, "Surf in the morning, drink beers in the afternoon when the guys are out. No problems."

My purpose in coming to Tahiti was to capture the mindset of the "average" Tahitian surfer. It seemed like a good idea when the topic was assigned to me by my editors back in California. But I found a mindset in flux, groups of surfers falling on both sides of an event, the discovery of the world's "heaviest wave," that was making inroads into the larger culture.

The expat American I met while surfing Papara Beach one morning had given that idea some thought during his years in Tahiti. Talking about the subject after our surf, he noticed a Tahitian friend of his preparing to paddle out. "See, this guy is the archetypal Tahitian surfer. An Australian gave him that piggy board 10 years ago and he's still riding it—and he rips the thing. He's a flight attendant on Tahiti Nui. When he's at home, he surfs here. When he's not at home, he's not thinking about surfing."

To Poto, surfing is always, even if dangerously, at the forefront. Before Teahupoo was revealed to the world, he paddled into big waves alone on a regular basis. There weren't many skis around then and big-wave surfing wasn't in vogue. His buddies didn't seem to be interested in the challenge, and Poto couldn't convince them to come along. Now, he said, the ideals of the big-wave charger have taken hold, and he surfs alone less frequently. I asked if he meant big waves at Teahupoo. He looked at me gravely and said, "There are other big-wave spots than Teahupoo. You do know that, right?"

Steinbeck's young fisherman, Kino, and his wife, Juana, ended up throwing the "pearl of the world" back into the sea it had come from. Juana knew the time before the pearl, "was gone, and there was no retrieving it. And knowing this, she abandoned the past instantly." Steinbeck wrote that the villagers all took their own meaning from the retelling of Kino's parable, which is heartening, considering that there is bound to be another "pearl of the world" out there. And who knows, there's a good chance some locals are sitting on it right now.

Fernando de Noronha

FELIPE WAS SITTING in the bushes, watching and waiting. He had his feral little friend with him, Calego, the one they called "Little Blond," the one who'd been living in a cave for five years. Felipe and Calego sat under the green canopy surrounded by lizards and ants for three hours. Then in a white-hot instant, Felipe snapped.

None of us knew that we were being watched. We paid no attention to the greenery behind the white sand beach or the great wall of black rock that rose from it. We'd walked down to this stretch of sand to escape a leftover World Qualifying Series crowd at Cacimba, the focal point of this tiny island.

The contest had ended a day earlier. What remained was a beach littered with amped mainland competitors and their frolicking girl-friends—beautiful slim-bikinied bodies in every shade from alabaster to black. Before their bright umbrellas and beach games, the thumping break looked something like a liquid-blue picnic sheet crawling with ants.

Opting to let the contest frenzy die out naturally, our crew of recently arrived Americans wandered down to an empty stretch peppered with a few peaks. A good spot to shoot photos, the boys thought. No big deal really. But unknown to us, Felipe had been sitting in the bushes, smoking weed with Little Blond and waiting for the tide—waiting for that precise moment.

Chris Ward, Dustin Barca, Nate Yeomans, Ian Rotgans, Cheyne Magnussen and Pat Maus paddled out. Photographer Jason Kenworthy followed in swim fins. The sizable pod of professionals began to dominate Felipe's chosen break just as the tide became optimal. The 42-year-old Brazilian in the bushes decided on patience at first. Then he waited uneasily, a bit miffed. And as the waves began to peel, he waited angrily for us to leave.

I noticed the deeply tanned surfer only when he came storming down the beach with his board, screaming and waving his free hand at the water, and then at me and Cheyne, who'd come in to change boards.

He howled at the guys in the water some more, and approaching us he screamed emphatically, "Tell your friends to leave. They surf three hours already. Tell them to go. This, Brazil! I like train easy. Tell the foreigners to leave."

Train easy? I wondered. Crazy talk.

Cheyne, who gaped at the madman slack-jawed, uttered wistfully, "What the fuck?"

Just then, right before me, Cheyne and a frantic Felipe, Chris free fell sideways into what looked certain to be an overhead closeout. His inside fin barely caught the bottom of the wave's trough. Just perceptibly swiveling his ankles, he pulled under a thick curtain. I was positive it would be another of the closeouts that had been pounding me into the sandbar. But Chris appeared again, deftly negotiated another two motley, heaving sections before squeaking out a slender doggie door 25 yards down the beach. As the Brazilians would say, "The wave didn't want him." Chris didn't seem to care. It was a display of surfing comparable only to something you might see at Oahu's Backdoor.

Cheyne and I watched in silence until the ride was over, and then Felipe began screaming again. I suppose Felipe thought that if he yelled enough, Cheyne or I might actually paddle out and halt the best display of surfing going on in the entire Atlantic Ocean at that moment. Instead, we just looked at the weather-beaten man, dumbfounded.

Finally, Felipe gave up on us, paddled out into the lineup and began screaming at our friends. Pat was just about to end his session. But with a fresh-looking tattoo across his collarbone that read, "You're either on my side, or in my way," there was no way he could. Dustin, who'd given the same orders plenty of times in Hawaii, wasn't about to accept the other end of localism. And Chris, seemingly oblivious, just kept pulling into impossible tubes.

Remarkably, a head-high wave stalled the dispute. Felipe stopped screaming long enough to paddle for its peak. He pulled in, and for a 42-year-old, rode the tube impressively well. Afterward, he paddled back out and screamed some more, until even he was bored with the tirade. Once he'd stopped his yammering, the boys felt secure enough in their toughness to call it a day. "I surfed six hours because of that guy," Chris muttered.

As THE WQS contestants filtered off the island on the once-a-day flights, our photo-collecting crew settled into a leisurely life at a little tiled guest house perched on the rise of a dirt road. From the road you could look left and see the "inner" ocean, you could look right and see the "outer" ocean. It didn't feel like living on an island, it felt like living on a boat.

A blustery wind careened down this dirt road every day. It picked up mid-morning, blowing off the southern Atlantic. It crested the rocky windward shore, passed our guest house, a few dirt lots, the ancient police station, the barren *supermercado*, the pecking hens, arrogant roosters, a feeble horse, a dune buggy or two, and continued through green, quaking trees and the stoic colonial town until it reached the island's leeward shore. There it sculpted blue-blue wave faces breaking across white sand beaches. This was enough for us, the foreign surfers who traveled absurd distances to get to this tiny spit of land, but not for the wind. It continued marching onward, past other islands, rumored offshore breaks and into the unknowable north.

The wind is everything here at this UNESCO world heritage site. It directs the Atlantic currents, which carry the rare turtles, sharks and fish from Africa. It brought the first Europeans, who brought a penal colony, a church and trees. It brought pirates, and it brought the U.S. army, who brought contractors, who brought the first surfer. This little volcanic spike of an island, rising out of the Atlantic just four degrees south of the equator and 215 miles off of the Brazilian coast, was shaped by the wind.

The only aspect of the island that seemed unimpressed by the wind was the spires of black rock rising as much as a thousand feet from the ocean. The tallest one, Pico Hill, was shaped undeniably, like a monstrous, erect penis. We wanted to reject the similarity but couldn't. The rock descended into a bulging scrotum and then into a lush, green undergrowth. Pat, the loudmouthed surfer from Carlsbad, California, and Noronha veteran, began giving directions to the beaches in respect to this formation, "Pass the cock and make a right," or "turn down the hill just before you get to the cock."

But just "the cock" was too crude, so its name evolved among us interlopers into "Cock Rock." The irony was that this island looked like it could have been Captain Hook's hideaway, replete with a dark mountain shaped like a foreboding skull. But, no, instead of a morbid skull, we got Cock Rock. Alternatively, Cacimba is hemmed in by a pair of giant rock orbs rising out of the surf. They looked, of course, like a mammoth pair of tits—nipples, too. One could be surfing next to the tits and look down to see Cock Rock thrusting into the sky. Obviously, the fertility of mating season on this tropical island had affected us. I asked Nate where he surfed one day, and he said, "Oh, just on that left that bounces off the tits."

JASON HAD ARRANGED this trip. He'd been here the year before and saw something in Fernando de Noronha's unique character that wavered beyond the physical possibilities he saw in it as a photographer. This year he'd been planning on training in Brazilian Jiu-jitsu at the Barra Gracie dojo in Rio, but was compelled to return to this distant island before he did. The timing fell within the parameters of the yearly WQS contest held on Noronha, so the surfers were easy to collect. I was just a tagalong, a writer easily lured to obscure islands.

Once here, though, I sensed that unknowable element Jason felt on his first trip. The island didn't hold the postcard-perfect beauty you might expect of a tropical island. It was a more exposed, more ragged beauty that mingled with it a sense of mystery. And although you'd imagine the feeling on an island this idyllic to be something nearing serenity, it produced a sense of otherness—a strange island so magnificent in its oceanic bounty that Jacques Cousteau made films here, spent months here. Maybe this feeling had to do with the *Papillion*-style penal colony whose walls still stood crumbling in the greenery. Maybe it was the century-old colonial town and battlements. Maybe it was just the frenzy of small life—birds, geckos, albino frogs, lizards, wild dogs and rats. Or, maybe it was just the wind. But regardless of cause, as Jason diligently set out to capture whatever this mystery was on film, I went out to find the people who knew something about it.

"Why haven't you been hanging out with us?" Pat asked,

confrontationally, waving a beer can at me. I'd arrived back at the guest house in the early evening and the afternoon beers were spilling over into the night. We could hear *forro* music bumping and jeering in the house next door and could sense the nighttime *partidos* beginning.

"I've just been cruising around, doing research," I said. I didn't add that I thought it a waste to travel thousands of miles to sit in a swampy guest house playing video games and watching DVDs. But I couldn't deride the lifestyle either. I was, as Pat pointed out, just like the rest of the crew: a beer-swilling vagabond surfer who'd gotten used to taking this lifestyle around the world with him. Still, I was surfing alone, too. The swell direction had changed in such a way as to make most every wave a horrid closeout. I'd been looking for something more ripable. These guys were professionals though and knew their work. The work consisted of photo sessions in which pulling into closeout barrels for the camera, "connecting" as they called it, meant something. They could visualize the images of themselves slotted in transparent blue waves printed on glossy four-color magazine pages.

The futile act of pulling into closeouts all day seemed ridiculous to me, and I said as much to Pat on the beach.

"Yeah," Pat said matter-of-factly. "Ripable is great and all, but I want some waves that make money."

Money-making waves—I had to think my way around that one while knowing full well that not hanging out to document those

moneymakers made me a jerk, maybe even remiss. The difference
between us, I told myself, was that I was a couple of years older
and a working journalist. But as Pat seemed to indicate, all this
really meant was that I was a loner who took my beer and surfboard with me while I chatted up the island's residents. Maybe
true, but there was an unknown element on this island I felt compelled to, maybe not investigate, but just come closer to under-
standing. Searching for a founding surfer here, I felt, might help
explain some of the mystery.

At one point I found myself sitting across from a marine biologist at the IBAMA offices. IBAMA is a governmental organization
that manages and studies the turtles and other rare sea life that
migrate here to breed. On the beach I'd seen the mounds of sand
turtles made to protect their eggs. But I hadn't seen any turtles.
So, I asked this sincere biologist about their absence. He waved to
a map of the island behind his desk, making an effort to speak
English for me. "Right now, the turtles are fucking around here."
He pointed to the spot. "They are fucking, fucking, fucking, and
then they return to the beach to lay eggs." He turned around to
see the wry smile on my face. "Oh, sorry, I say 'fuck,' because I
forget this other word."

"No," I said. "'Fucking' is more precise."

In a bar, I met young IBAMA volunteers who loved their work
and knew how lucky they were to spend each season here. A volunteer in her early 20s, Juli, said, "OK, there are other places in Brazil

that are as beautiful as this, near Rio, for example. But here you can just be, without that fear around you."

One of her friends added what this mainland fear was: "Wise guys. Guys always looking around for an opportunity." But Fernando de Noronha, because of its isolation and its prohibitive expense for the average Brazilian, remained separate from these third-world dangers. One could safely sleep on the beach, the volunteers pointed out, or walk home in the dark.

The volunteers took me to other bars and introduced me to their friends. They taught me how to say, "You are very beautiful," in Portuguese. They tried to teach me the three-step dance that *forro* music required. One of the girls said that *forro* music was brought to northern Brazil by a polka-playing American. The name was based on the English words "for all." The girl smiled and said, "Music 'for all' people." The guys of the group tried to fill me in on the nature of Brazilian women. One said, "The women are like boomerangs. They leave you, go about the room, but they always come back. They don't like for you to chase them." An older guy, obviously acknowledging the class differences of Brazilian society, said, "Women don't like men. Queers like men. Women like money." We laughed.

The group of us walked back to one of their guest houses and sat on the porch under a massive tree. We could hear the flitting music of the bars and the croaking frogs. Someone rolled a joint, and I talked about surfing with the guys as the girls rapped softly in

Portuguese. The guys confirmed that Noronha had the best and heaviest beachbreak in Brazil—powerful like Puerto Escondido, Mexico, but smaller. They lamented how expensive it was to get here. Then one of them subtly mentioned that the first Brazilian to ever surf Noronha, a surfer named Dantas, was staying nearby.

BACK AT OUR guest house, Pat asked the question he was burning to ask for days now. "Are you gonna write about the riders, or the island?"

"The island," I said.

"What? Some Sam-George-feathering-offshores-ominous-waves-and-beautiful-sunset piece of shit? Why don't you write a story about us? You've got such a group of characters here. This ain't no regular Joe Curren trip. Why don't you write the real life of pro surfers—drinkin' beer and fuckin' bitches!" He raised his beer can and howled. All of the English speakers laughed.

That night 28-year-old Pat verbally tormented the younger surfers Ian, Cheyne and Nate. Then he challenged them to Jiu-jitsu grappling matches, which led to broken furniture. The ladies who ran the guest house came complaining to me because I spoke Spanish and a few Portuguese words. I didn't know what to tell them. I didn't really care.

The next night Pat went on the offensive again, but this time Jason put his foot down and "choked-out" Pat until he puked and blacked out. Filling in downtime with action is the "real" story of pro surfers on the road, whatever that action may be. The next day we grinned over the truth of it as Jason, the head of this mob, admitted, "I don't think I could do this job if I didn't train hard in Jiu-jitsu."

"COME WITH US. It will be good for you."

I'd found the address of Noronha's founding surfer through a talkative American who'd overheard my desire to speak with this guy named Dantas. Apparently, the American had chatted up everybody on the island until I was presented a rough address late one night at the Dog Bar. The next morning I drove down to the area described and parked the buggy at the side of the road next to a green open field where a shabby white horse picked at grass. The other side of the road was crowded with guest houses, and I began walking toward them when an older Brazilian surfer, a short, wild-looking blond man, and a tall woman stepped off of a porch and began walking toward me. "Hey, there you are," said the surfer.

In the way of islanders everywhere, this man Dantas knew that I was coming before it had occurred to me to come. But, ambling closer, I recognized the man and stopped in my tracks. It was Felipe from the beach, angry Felipe Dantas, and he had Little Blond with him. I didn't take another step. I considered my options. They continued toward me.

I sucked it up. I cautiously introduced myself. And then I began to explain my visit when Felipe said, "Yes, I know." He added plainly, "Come with us, it will be good for you."

I looked at the three of them. Felipe appeared nearly serene now, but like a puppy, Little Blond could barely stand in one place. The woman at their side, Tatiana, her green eyes fluttering under dark lashes, was easily as beautiful a woman as I'd ever seen. Felipe waved down the road, and I was so stunned by the sight of them, I could only follow.

A hundred yards down the road we turned onto a bush trail and walked into the trees, a canopy unfolded over our heads. Little Blond began jabbering in Portuguese and ran off the trail, into and out of the trees. "He's named Calego," Felipe said. "We call him 'Little Blond.' He live in a cave five years. He's a little crazy." Felipe pointed to his own head and rolled his eyes. Tatiana strolled ahead of us, elegantly brushing branches out of her way. I could have been interviewing Tarzan, Jane and their little blond chimp. Felipe pointed out the Donkey Milk trees, moss and lichens. Tatiana held vines for us and Calego ran back to the trail with arms full of mangos.

We hiked up an incline and found ourselves before two great rocks. A pathway led between them. "This where the army come up to survey island," Felipe said. I followed Tatiana through them, and into the sunlight again where we ascended increasingly large boulders. Without prompting, Felipe began talking about his life abroad and here on Noronha. He'd tried his luck at surfing professionally, and in 1994 was rated 52 on the WQS. He'd lived in

Hawaii for a stint, and back in Sao Paulo, he worked in their blooming surf industry. I'd gathered that he'd been returning to Noronha throughout that period.

Tatiana led us farther up, and through a break in the rocks, I could finally see how high we'd climbed. Cacimba lay like a flash of white below us, the blue of the Atlantic extending forever northward. With all fours we scuttled up a final boulder until we could climb no farther. I suddenly realized where we were—smack dab on the crown of Cock Rock's bulbous scrotum. The shaft of Cock Rock rose like a black tower beside us. The island stretched out below, rippling green bush and black rock, until it broke into crumbs adrift in the ocean. Just then, Calego came scampering up the rock with a wild grin beneath his beard; he saw a bird hovering over us in the southeasterly wind, and it amazed him.

Felipe pointed to a chain ladder that ascended Cock Rock. His father's company had built it through contract work with the military. That was in 1976, and when his father returned to the mainland, he told Felipe about the waves he saw on Noronha. Felipe returned with his father on subsequent visits, and once he was old enough, he spent weeks sailing here with friends. It was on that sailboat trip in 1987 that Felipe was photographed for the cover of *Fluid* magazine, and the cat was out of the bag for Fernando de Noronha.

We looked out to the expanse of the sea. Felipe told me about a man Jacques Cousteau had named "Man of the Sea." The native had lived off the island and could free dive to untold depths, amazing Cousteau's film crew. Felipe mentioned other islands nearby and big-wave breaks off shore. Up on that rock, I remembered asking the IBAMA marine biologist where the baby turtles go after they hatch. "Out in the sea," he said. "No one knows where."

Taking in the breadth of the ocean around us, I could understand why only one hatchling in a thousand make it back here.

AFTER TATIANA MADE juice from the mangos Calego collected, we sat on the porch of their guest house and Felipe talked about the future of young Brazilian pros. If they don't come to places like this, or train somewhere else in heavy waves, they won't get anywhere, he said. It seemed natural that a conversation about his discovery of Noronha's surf would lead to the future of Brazilian surfing.

On leaving, I felt the maelstrom of ideas that come after interviewing uniquely intense people. I decided to drive down to the beach for a surf before scribbling my notes. I parked the buggy on the sand and watched as closeout after closeout pounded the beach. The size had increased with the same result. It was a beautiful day though, and I felt lucky. Maybe, I'd make it out of one of those freight-training barrels. After I'd made the lineup, it took all of 30 minutes for the relentless closeouts to pummel me into submission. The luck I'd felt must have been the idea that I could make it back to the beach without smashing anything.

The boys pulled up in another buggy as I walked up the beach.

In the harsh glare of the midday sun, I watched them grab their boards and run for the lines of whitewater. Jason followed, walking backward into the surf with his swim fins and water housing. I was loading my board into the buggy and wasn't paying attention to one of Cheyne's initial waves. As I learned later, he dropped in, pulled under the lip and raced the barrel until he watched the wave go absolutely dry beneath him. He dove forward, landed on the dry sandbar and heard his collar bone snap.

As a true professional, he didn't complain or whine as he exited the surf, cradling his arm so that his collarbone wouldn't move. It was all part of the work. Once he was loaded into the buggy, Pat asked, "Do you mind if only Nate goes with you so the rest of us can stay and get some shots?" Cheyne agreed—it was the work after all—and he went with Nate to the half-ass medical clinic, received a sling and a handful of aspirin. The next day Cheyne began the first of five long flights home alone.

AT SOME STAGE, and I don't know when, Pat and I came to terms with each other—the pro surfer and the surf journalist. We were nearly the same age, both raised in Southern California and we'd both been around the world doing the thing we loved. So, we found ourselves drinking beers together on the porch of our guest house on a lazy Sunday afternoon. We watched the wind wiping up dust in the road and listened to a rooster crow. I don't know what we were talking about, but at a certain moment, Pat looked out

across the dirt lots before us and focused on the ancient police station. It didn't look much different than the old penal colony rotting in the bushes a quarter mile away.

"You know," he said reflectively. "I spent a few days in there last
year." Apparently, Pat had gotten shit-faced one night and decided
to tear around the island in his rental dune buggy. He missed a
corner near the guest house and crashed the buggy into somebody's yard. When the dust cleared and he realized what had happened, he got out and ran on foot back to the guest house, leaving
the smashed buggy where it had stopped. The police found him
there in the morning.

I peered over at the police station's foot thick walls and the iron
bars built into the cell windows. "It was gnarly," he said. "I looked
through the bars in my cell and could see the guys I'd come with
packing up over here. A bus came to take them to the airport, and
I was stuck there. I screamed, 'No! No!' I begged the police captain to let me go, but he's like, 'No, you stay.'"

We took sips off our beers, and then Pat had his bright idea.
"Let's go over there."

"Why?" I asked.

"I want you to see the cells. It would be good for your article."
There was an awkward pause. I didn't want to go. But then I
thought, I've gone to this length, I was leaving the next day; why
not check out the cells? We walked across the dirt lots with beers in
hand as though we'd wandered off from some tailgate party. The

jailhouse was painted a dirty yellow, there were old cannons mounted outside of it, and the scene was oddly quiet. As we approached the door, I could see two policemen inside its dirty interior. They looked at us as they would a couple of the mangy wild dogs running around, but it was too late to pretend we were looky-loos. Pat said, "Hey, we want to take a look at the cells."

Stupid, stupid, stupid, I thought. The policemen just stared at us. "This guy," Pat pointed at me, "he's a surf journalist doing an article on Fernando de Noronha. I want him to see the cells here."

The policeman at the desk said, "No spick English." Then, picking up the phone, he said, "You wait." He talked on the phone for a few minutes and set its receiver into the cradle. "You wait," he said again. "The captain comes."

Pat's face went slack as though he'd just remembered a terrible secret. I could see that sentence, "The captain comes," ringing around in his head.

"Dude, I can't be here. I gotta go. I never paid the fine, if the captain sees me, I'm done."

"OK," I said a bit relieved. "Let's go then." And I turned to walk back to the guest house that stood clearly in sight.

"No, dude, you gotta stay," Pat said, grabbing my arm. "If the captain comes, and you're not here, they'll come over to the guest house, and then I'm done."

I didn't want to stay. This wasn't my idea. And I couldn't imagine how seeing dirty third-world jail cells would be good for my article. But then, Pat had a point, he couldn't stay, I couldn't go. "OK," I said bitterly.

"Thanks, dude," Pat said. And I watched as he scampered back across the dirt lot.

I ditched my beer, but didn't have to wait long for the police captain to arrive. Once he did, I could see why Pat had abandoned me. The captain was big, dark and ugly—his carameled eyes peered from a pockmarked face. The captain conferred with his subordinates briefly before turning to confront me. "Why do you want to see the cells?" It was a thick, guttural voice. He folded his arms as he stepped up close.

"Oh, I'm writing an article about Fernando de Noronha and I was…I was just looking around." The captain looked me up and down, and then he looked at the sky.

"You write about the surfing?" he asked. Apparently his subordinates spoke more English than we thought.

"Yes," I said.

"Why don't you want to talk to surfers?" he asked. And, in this question, I saw my out as clear as day.

"I do. I want to talk to the local surfers. In fact, I'll just head down to the beach right now."

"No, you stay," he said, looking at the wind. "The surfers are not at the beach now. I will find the surfers for you. Then, you pay me," he said.

I thought this last bit over awhile. "Well, here's the thing: it's against journalistic ethics for me to pay for interviews. So I can't pay money to speak with the surfers," I said. He leaned closer, obviously choosing his words.

"I am only a police captain. We don't make much money. You pay me."

By the look in his yellow eyes and his stance just inches away from mine, I understood. I would pay him, or I would see the inside of one of his cells after all. I imagined looking through the bars and watching Pat, Jason, Ian and Nate being carried off to the airport. I'd be done.

"Well," I said. "Now is not a good time for me."

"When is a good time for you?" he scoffed.

"Tuesday would be fine," I said, knowing full well that I'd be leaving the next morning, Monday. The captain moved his head from side to side as he considered the transaction.

"OK," he agreed. "Tuesday. Then you pay me."

I just turned and walked back to the guest house, my head down as I wondered if the bus to the airport would arrive before this police captain and his subordinates did. That night I packed hopefully, desperately actually, now that I'd considered the implications of my deceit. The phone rang through the hall of the guesthouse. One of the house ladies came to my room and said that I had a telephone call. Odd, I thought, nobody but nobody could know where to reach me. I picked up the phone. It was the police captain. "I have surfers for you to talk to," he said.

"OK, great."

"Why don't you talk to them tomorrow. It's better for me."

"No," I said. "Tomorrow is no good. Tuesday is better."

"OK. Tuesday. Then you pay me."

"Thanks for calling," I said as I hung up.

It's hard to describe how beautiful that island looked to me—its green and black standing like a resolute way station in the Atlantic—as I sailed over it in a jet plane bound for the mainland, having not quite plumbed the mystery I'd felt there, but having not seen it through the inside of the captain's jail cell either.

For more photos and a glossary of foreign phrases, go to
www.KimballTaylor.com